THE RESISTING
READER

THE RESISTING READER

A Feminist Approach to
American Fiction

Judith Fetterley

INDIANA UNIVERSITY PRESS
Bloomington

An earlier version of Chapter 2 first appeared in Arlyn Diamond and Lee
Edwards, eds., *The Authority of Experience: Essays in Feminist Criticism,*
copyright © 1977 by The University of Massachusetts Press.

Manufactured in the United States of America

Library of Congress Cataloging in Publication Data
Fetterley, Judith, 1938-
The resisting reader.
Includes bibliographical references.
1. American fiction—History and criticism.
2. Women in literature.   3. Feminism and literature.
I. Title.
PS374.W6F4   813'.009'352   78-3242
ISBN 0-253-31078-4

4 5 6 7 8 93 92 91 90 89

Contents

*This book is lovingly dedicated to the
following women, with whom it all began:
Rosalie Davies, Elizabeth Gay Forbes,
Deborah Harris, Rosemary Hennessey,
Nancy Polikoff, Joann Ross, Linda Steiner*

PREFACE

This book began in the classroom. During the fall of 1971 I taught a course at the University of Pennsylvania entitled "Images of Women in American Literature." I asked the students in the course to keep a journal in which they were to record their responses to the literature we were reading and to our class discussions of it, and I indicated that I too was keeping such a journal. At the end of the semester when I asked to see their journals, the class quite reasonably asked to see mine, and the result was a fifteen-page, single-spaced document suggesting what I felt to be the central insights we had gained in relation to each book we had read. I distributed my "journal" to the students, to colleagues at the University of Pennsylvania, to various discussion groups at that year's MLA meetings, and to local feminist friends. The response was so enthusiastic and supportive that I felt I could undertake the project of developing the notes into a full-length study. I asked for and received a leave of absence, without pay, from the University of Pennsylvania for the following academic year, 1972–73, and I began the task that has occupied most of my time and energy for the past five years. I was finally able to complete my book, somewhat condensed from the original project, during the summer of 1975 with the aid of a Faculty Research Fellowship from the SUNY/Research Foundation.

The dialogue begun in that classroom at Penn has continued at SUNY/Albany, where I have for the past several years been teaching a course similar to the one I taught at Penn. In my classes I have continued to develop, refine, and change my ideas through interaction and exchange with my students. It is my sincere wish that this book will extend that dialogue even further and that it will be itself a form of teaching. Feminist criticism is a growing, changing, constantly self-transforming phenomenon characterized by a resistance to codification and a refusal to be rigidly defined or to have its parameters prematurely set. My introduction is an attempt to document those aspects of feminist criticism which have shaped my thinking and produced my book. It is not meant to be a definitive statement on the form and function of feminist criticism. As for my analyses of the literature, with each work there is much more that could be said, should be said, and, if the book works, will be said. I hope my book will be suggestive—that it will stimulate dialogue, discussion, debate, re-reading, and finally re-vision.

But, as Adrienne Rich has said, this "re-vision—the act of looking back, of seeing with fresh eyes, of entering an old text from a new critical direction—is for us more than a chapter in cultural history; it is an act of survival." My book is for me more than an academic matter, more than an act of literary criticism, more than a possible text for courses on women in American literature, more even than the source of dialogue; it is an act of survival. It is based on the premise that we read and that what we read affects us—drenches us, to use Rich's language, in its assumptions, and that to avoid drowning in this drench of assumptions we must learn to re-read. Thus, I see my book as a self-defense survival manual for the woman reader lost in "the masculine wilderness of the American novel." At its best, feminist criticism is a political act whose aim is not simply to interpret the world but to change it by changing the consciousness of those who read and their relation to what they read. In this sense I want my book to be, in the words of Suzanne Juhasz, "itself an event and not a comment upon an event" and to fulfill the charge of Andrea Dworkin: "I want writers to write books because they are committed to the content of those books. I want writers to write books as actions. I want writers to write books that can make a difference in how, and even why, people live. I want writers to write books that are worth being jailed for, worth fighting for, and should it come to that in this country, worth dying for."

And yet, of course, this study began long before that classroom at Penn, long before my commitment to feminism, long before I became a student of literature, long before my own birth. It began with the beginning of patriarchy and with the consequences of that system for women:

> A loss of something ever felt I—
> The first that I could recollect
> Bereft I was—of what I knew not
> Too young that any should suspect
>
> A Mourner walked among the children
> I notwithstanding went about
> As one bemoaning a Dominion
> Itself the only Prince cast out—

In the first two stanzas of this poem Dickinson has defined the condition of woman in patriarchal culture. Her primal act of consciousness is the sense of loss, a phenomenon that Freud in his massive phallocentrism arrogantly analyzed as a lament for a specific bit of flesh rather than for the possibilities of personhood which it represents. Bereft, disinherited, cast out, woman is the Other, the Outsider, a mourner among children; never really child because never allowed to be fully self-indulgent; never really adult because never permitted to be fully responsible; forever a "young mourner," a "little woman"; superhuman, subhuman but never simply human. Yet, worse even than the loss is the confusion of consciousness which obscures the nature of the loss and often the fact of loss itself. Hemmed about with myths and images and dogmas and definitions and laws and strictures and God and Man, and *fear* and *fear* and *fear,* she is deceived into believing the theory about the bit of flesh and the bite of apple and is kept from knowing of what she is bereft. Her condition is isolation, conviction of being "itself the only Prince cast out"; and her self-image is monstrous because that is the consequence of isolation. And because that is the consequence of the patriarchal predication that to be human is to be male. The condition of woman under patriarchy is precisely that of a prince cast out. Forced in every way to identify with men, yet incessantly reminded of being woman, she undergoes a transformation into an "it," the dominion of personhood lost indeed.

My book, then, is dedicated to the definition of our loss, the dissolution of our solitude, and the reclaiming of our dominion.

It has been, therefore, an understandably communal act made possible by the energy and vision of countless women who have encouraged and assisted and inspired. One part of my deepest debt has been realized by the dedication; another part has been realized in my introductory chapter, where the extensive quoting serves not simply to establish points or to share important perceptions but to express the degree of my indebtedness to the work of other women; the final part I realize now in thanking those women who in particular have given generously of their time and energy, emotional and intellectual, to the process of writing this book: Martha Warn Firestine, Carole Friedman, and Joan Schulz.

INTRODUCTION
On the Politics of Literature

I

Literature is political. It is painful to have to insist on this fact, but the necessity of such insistence indicates the dimensions of the problem. John Keats once objected to poetry "that has a palpable design upon us." The major works of American fiction constitute a series of designs on the female reader, all the more potent in their effect because they are "impalpable." One of the main things that keeps the design of our literature unavailable to the consciousness of the woman reader, and hence impalpable, is the very posture of the apolitical, the pretense that literature speaks universal truths through forms from which all the merely personal, the purely subjective, has been burned away or at least transformed through the medium of art into the representative. When only one reality is encouraged, legitimized, and transmitted and when that limited vision endlessly insists on its comprehensiveness, then we have the conditions necessary for that confusion of consciousness in which impalpability flourishes. It is the purpose of this book to give voice to a different reality and different vision, to bring a different subjectivity to bear on the old "universality." To examine American fictions in light of how attitudes toward women shape their form and content is to make available to consciousness that which has been largely left unconscious and thus to change our understanding of these fictions, our relation to them, and their effect on us. It is to make palpable their designs.

American literature is male. To read the canon of what is currently considered classic American literature is perforce to identify as male. Though exceptions to this generalization can be found here and there—a Dickinson poem, a Wharton novel—these exceptions usually function to obscure the argument and confuse the issue: American literature is male. Our literature neither leaves women alone nor allows them to participate. It insists on its universality at the same time that it defines that universality in specifically male terms. "Rip Van Winkle" is paradigmatic of this phenomenon. While the desire to avoid work, escape authority, and sleep through the major decisions of one's life is obviously applicable to both men and women, in Irving's story this "universal" desire is made specifically male. Work, authority, and decision-making are symbolized by Dame Van Winkle, and the longing for flight is defined against her. She is what one must escape from, and the "one" is necessarily male. In Mailer's *An American Dream*, the fantasy of eliminating all one's ills through the ritual of scapegoating is equally male: the sacrificial scapegoat is the woman/wife and the cleansed survivor is the husband/male. In such fictions the female reader is co-opted into participation in an experience from which she is explicitly excluded; she is asked to identify with a selfhood that defines itself in opposition to her; she is required to identify against herself.

The woman reader's relation to American literature is made even more problematic by the fact that our literature is frequently dedicated to defining what is peculiarly American about experience and identity. Given the pervasive male bias of this literature, it is not surprising that in it the experience of being American is equated with the experience of being male. In Fitzgerald's *The Great Gatsby*, the background for the experience of disillusionment and betrayal revealed in the novel is the discovery of America, and Daisy's failure of Gatsby is symbolic of the failure of America to live up to the expectations in the imagination of the men who "discovered" it. America is female; to be American is male; and the quintessential American experience is betrayal by woman. Henry James certainly defined our literature, if not our culture, when he picked the situation of women as the subject of *The Bostonians,* his very American tale.

Power is the issue in the politics of literature, as it is in the politics of anything else. To be excluded from a literature that claims to define one's identity is to experience a peculiar form of powerlessness—not simply the powerlessness which derives from not seeing one's experience articulated, clarified, and legitimized in art, but more significantly the powerlessness which results from the endless division of self against self, the consequence of the invocation to identify as male while being reminded that to be male—to be universal, to be American—is to be *not female.* Not only does powerlessness characterize woman's experience of reading, it also describes the content of what is read. Each of the works chosen for this study presents a version and an enactment of the drama of men's power over women. The final irony, and indignity, of the woman reader's relation to American literature, then, is that she is required to dissociate herself from the very experience the literature engenders. Powerlessness is the subject and powerlessness the experience, and the design insists that Rip Van Winkle/Frederic Henry/Nick Carraway/Stephen Rojack speak for us all.

The drama of power in our literature is often disguised. In "Rip Van Winkle," Rip poses as powerless, the henpecked husband cowering before his termagant Dame. Yet, when Rip returns from the mountains, armed by the drama of female deposition witnessed there, to discover that his wife is dead and he is free to enjoy what he has always wanted, the "Shucks, M'am, I don't mean no harm" posture dissolves. In Sherwood Anderson's "I Want to Know Why," the issue of power is refracted through the trauma of a young boy's discovery of what it means to be male in a culture that gives white men power over women, horses, and niggers. More sympathetic and honest than "Rip," Anderson's story nevertheless exposes both the imaginative limits of our literature and the reasons for those limits. Storytelling and art can do no more than lament the inevitable—boys must grow up to be men; it can provide no alternative vision of being male. Bathed in nostalgia, "I Want to Know Why" is infused with the perspective it abhors, because finally to disavow that perspective would be to relinquish power. The lament is self-indulgent; it offers the luxury of feeling bad without the responsibility of change. And it is completely male-centered, registering the tragedy of sexism through its cost to men. At the end we cry for the boy and not for the whores he will eventually make use of.

In Hawthorne's "The Birthmark," the subject of power is more explicit. The fact of men's power over women and the full implications of that fact are the crux of the story. Aylmer is free to experiment on Georgiana, to the point of death, because she is both woman and wife. Hawthorne indicates the attractiveness of the power that marriage puts in the hands of men through his description of Aylmer's reluctance to leave his laboratory and through his portrayal of Aylmer's inherent discomfort with women and sex. And why does Aylmer want this power badly enough to overcome his initial reluctance and resistance? Hitherto Aylmer has failed in all his efforts to achieve a power equal to that of "Mother" nature. Georgiana provides an opportunity for him to outdo nature by remaking her creation. And if he fails, he still will have won because he will have destroyed the earthly embodiment and repre-

sentative of his adversary. Hawthorne intends his character to be seen as duplicitous, and he maneuvers Aylmer
through the poses of lover, husband, and scientist to show
us how Aylmer attempts to gain power and to use that
power to salve his sense of inadequacy. But even so,
Hawthorne, like Anderson, is unwilling to do more with
the sickness than call it sick. He obscures the issue of sexual
politics behind a haze of "universals" and clothes the murder of wife by husband in the language of idealism.

Though the grotesque may serve Faulkner as a disguise
in the same way that the ideal serves Hawthorne, "A Rose
for Emily" goes farther than "The Birthmark" in making
the power of men over women an overt subject. Emily's life
is shaped by her father's absolute control over her; her
murder of Homer Barron is *re*action, not action. Though
Emily exercises the power the myths of sexism make available to her, that power is minimal; her retaliation is no
alternative to the patriarchy which oppresses her. Yet
Faulkner, like Anderson and Hawthorne, ultimately protects himself and short-circuits the implications of his
analysis, not simply through the use of the grotesque,
which makes Emily eccentric rather than central, but also
through his choice of her victim. In having Emily murder
Homer Barron, a northern day-laborer, rather than Judge
Stevens, the southern patriarch, Faulkner indicates how
far he is willing to go in imagining even the minimal reversal of power involved in retaliation. The elimination of
Homer Barron is no real threat to the system Judge Stevens represents. Indeed, a few day-laborers may have to be
sacrificed here and there to keep that system going.

In *A Farewell to Arms,* the issue of power is thoroughly
obscured by the mythology, language, and structure of
romantic love and by the invocation of an abstract, though
spiteful, "they" whose goal it is to break the good, the
beautiful, and the brave. Yet the brave who is broken is
Catherine; at the end of the novel Catherine is dead, Fred-

eric is alive, and the resemblance to "Rip Van Winkle" and "The Birthmark" is unmistakable. Though the scene in the hospital is reminiscent of Aylmer's last visit to Georgiana in her chambers, Hemingway, unlike Hawthorne, separates his protagonist from the source of his heroine's death, locating the agency of Catherine's demise not simply in "them" but in her biology. Frederic survives several years of war, massive injuries, the dangers of a desperate retreat, and the threat of execution by his own army; Catherine dies in her first pregnancy. Clearly, biology is destiny. Yet, Catherine is as much a scapegoat as Dame Van Winkle, Georgiana, Daisy Fay, and Deborah Rojack. For Frederic to survive, free of the intolerable burdens of marriage, family, and fatherhood, yet with his vision of himself as the heroic victim of cosmic antagonism intact, Catherine must die. Frederic's necessities determine Catherine's fate. He is, indeed, the agent of her death.

In its passionate attraction to the phenomenon of wealth, *The Great Gatsby* reveals its author's consuming interest in the issue of power. In the quintessentially male drama of poor boy's becoming rich boy, ownership of women is invoked as the index of power: he who possesses Daisy Fay is the most powerful boy. But when the rich boy, fearing finally for his territory, repossesses the girl and, by asking "Who is he," strips the poor boy of his presumed power, the resultant animus is directed not against the rich boy but against the girl, whose rejection of him exposes the poor boy's powerlessness. The struggle for power between men is deflected into safer and more certain channels, and the consequence is the familiar demonstration of male power over women. This demonstration, however, is not simply the result of a greater safety in directing anger at women than at men. It derives as well from the fact that even the poorest male gains something from a system in which all women are at some level his subjects. Rather than attack the men who represent and manifest that system, he identifies with them and acquires his sense of power through superiority to women. It is not surprising, therefore, that the drama of *The Great Gatsby* involves an attack on Daisy, whose systematic reduction from the glamorous object of Gatsby's romantic longings to the casual killer of Myrtle Wilson provides an accurate measure of the power available to the most "powerless" male.

By his choice of scene, context, and situation, Henry James in *The Bostonians* directly confronts the hostile nature of the relations between men and women and sees in that war the defining characteristics of American culture. His honesty provides the opportunity for a clarification rather than a confusion of consciousness and offers a welcome relief from the deceptions of other writers. Yet the drama, while correctly labeled, is still the same. *The Bostonians* is an unrelenting demonstration of the extent, and an incisive analysis of the sources, of the power of men as a class over women as a class. Yet, though James laments women's oppression, and laments it because of its effects *on women,* he nevertheless sees it as inevitable. *The Bostonians* represents a kind of end point in the literary exploration of sex/class power; it would be impossible to see more clearly and feel more deeply and still remain convinced that patriarchy is inevitable. Indeed, there is revolution latent in James's novel, and, while he would be the last to endorse it, being far more interested in articulating and romanticizing the tragic elements in women's powerlessness, *The Bostonians* provides the material for that analysis of American social reality which is the beginning of change.

Norman Mailer's *An American Dream* represents another kind of end point. Mailer is thoroughly enthralled by the possibility of power that sexism makes available to men, absolutely convinced that he is in danger of losing it, and completely dedicated to maintaining it, at whatever cost. It is impossible to imagine a more frenzied commitment to the maintenance of male power than Mailer's. In *An American Dream* all content has been reduced to the enactment of men's power over women, and to the development and legitimization of that act Mailer brings every strategy he can muster, not the least of which is an extended elaboration of the mythology of female power. In Mailer's work the effort to obscure the issue, disguise reality, and confuse consciousness is so frantic that the antitheses he provides to protect his thesis become in fact his message and his confusions shed a lurid illumination. If *The Bostonians* induces one to rearrange James's conceptual framework and so to make evitable his inevitable, *An American Dream* induces a desire to eliminate Mailer's conceptual framework altogether and start over. Beyond his frenzy is only utter nausea and weariness of spirit and a profound willingness to give up an exhausted, sick, and sickening struggle. In Mailer, the drama of power comes full circle; at once the most sexist writer, he is also the most freeing, and out of him it may be possible to create anew.

II

But what have I to say of *Sexual Politics* itself? Millett has undertaken a task which I find particularly worthwhile: the consideration of certain events or works of literature from an unexpected, even startling point of view. Millett never suggests that hers is a sufficient analysis of any of the works she discusses. Her aim is to wrench the reader from the vantage point he has long occupied, and force him to look at life and letters from a new coign. Hers is not meant to be the last word on any writer, but a wholly new word, little heard before and strange. For the first time we have been asked to look at literature as women; we, men, women and Ph.D.'s, have always read it as men. Who cannot point to a certain over-emphasis in the way Millett reads Lawrence or Stalin or Euripides. What matter? We are rooted in our vantage points and require transplanting which, always dangerous, involves violence and the possibility of death.

—*Carolyn Heilbrun*[1]

The method that is required is not one of correlation but of *liberation*. Even the term "method" must be reinterpreted and in fact wrenched out of its usual semantic field, for the emerging creativity in women is by no means a merely cerebral process. In order to understand the implications of this process it is necessary to grasp the fundamental fact that women have had the power of *naming* stolen from us. We have not been free to use our own power to name ourselves, the world, or God. The old naming was not the product of dialogue—a fact inadvertently admitted in the Genesis story of Adam's naming the animals and the woman. Women are now realizing that the universal imposing of names by men has been false because partial. That is, inadequate words have been taken as adequate.   —*Mary Daly*[2]

Re-vision—the act of looking back, of seeing with fresh eyes, of entering an old text from a new critical direction—is for us more than a chapter in cultural history: it is an act of survival. Until we can understand the assumptions in which we are drenched we cannot know ourselves. And this drive to self-knowledge, for woman, is more than a search for identity: it is part of her refusal of the self-destructiveness of male-dominated society. A radical critique of literature, feminist in its impulse, would take the work first of all as a clue to how we live, how we have been living, how we have been led to imagine ourselves, how our language has trapped as well as liberated us; and how we can begin to see—and therefore live—afresh.   —*Adrienne Rich*[3]

A culture which does not allow itself to look clearly at the obvious through the universal accessibility of art is a culture of tragic delusion, hardly viable.   —*Cynthia Ozick*[4]

When a system of power is thoroughly in command, it has scarcely need to speak itself aloud; when its workings are exposed and questioned, it becomes not only subject to discussion, but even to change.   —*Kate Millett*[5]

Consciousness is power. To create a new understanding of our literature is to make possible a new effect of that literature on us. And to make possible a new effect is in turn to provide the conditions for changing the culture that the literature reflects. To expose and question that complex of ideas and mythologies about women and men which exist in our society and are confirmed in our literature is to make the system of power embodied in the literature open not only to discussion but even to change. Such questioning and exposure can, of course, be carried on only by a consciousness radically different from the one that informs the literature. Such a closed system cannot be opened up from within but only from without. It must be entered into from a point of view which questions its values and assumptions and which has its investment in making available to consciousness precisely that which the literature wishes to keep hidden. Feminist criticism provides that point of view and embodies that consciousness.

In "A Woman's Map of Lyric Poetry," Elizabeth Hampsten, after quoting in full Thomas Campion's "My Sweetest Lesbia," asks, "And Lesbia, what's in it for her?"[6] The answer to this question is the subject of Hampsten's essay and the answer is, of course, nothing. But implicit in her question is another answer—a great deal, for someone. As Lillian Robinson reminds us, "and, always, *cui bono*— who profits?"[7] The questions of who profits, and how, are crucial because the attempt to answer them leads directly to an understanding of the function of literary sexual politics. Function is often best known by effect. Though one of the most persistent of literary stereotypes is the castrating bitch, the cultural reality is not the emasculation of men by women but the *immasculation* of women by men. As readers and teachers and scholars, women are taught to think as men, to identify with a male point of view, and to accept as normal and legitimate a male system of values, one of whose central principles is misogyny.

One of the earliest statements of the phenomenon of immasculation, serving indeed as a position paper, is

Elaine Showalter's "Women and the Literary Curriculum."
In the opening part of her article, Showalter imaginatively
recreates the literary curriculum the average young
woman entering college confronts:

> In her freshman year she would probably study literature
> and composition, and the texts in her course would be
> selected for their timeliness, or their relevance, or their
> power to involve the reader, rather than for their absolute
> standing in the literary canon. Thus she might be assigned
> any one of the texts which have recently been advertised for
> Freshman English: an anthology of essays, perhaps such as
> *The Responsible Man*, "for the student who wants literature
> relevant to the world in which he lives," or *Conditions of Men*,
> or *Man in Crisis: Perspectives on The Individual and His World*,
> or again, *Representative Men: Cult Heroes of Our Time*, in
> which thirty-three men represent such categories of
> heroism as the writer, the poet, the dramatist, the artist, and
> the guru, and the only two women included are the Actress
> Elizabeth Taylor and The Existential Heroine Jacqueline
> Onassis. . . . By the end of her freshman year, a woman
> student would have learned something about intellectual
> neutrality; she would be learning, in fact, how to think like a
> man.[8]

Showalter's analysis of the process of immasculation raises
a central question: "What are the effects of this long ap-
prenticeship in negative capability on the self-image and
the self-confidence of women students?" And the answer is
self-hatred and self-doubt: "Women are estranged from
their own experience and unable to perceive its shape and
authenticity. . . . they are expected to identify as readers
with a masculine experience and perspective, which is
presented as the human one. . . . Since they have no faith
in the validity of their own perceptions and experiences,
rarely seeing them confirmed in literature, or accepted in
criticism, can we wonder that women students are so often

timid, cautious, and insecure when we exhort them to 'think for themselves'?"[9]

The experience of immasculation is also the focus of Lee Edwards' article, "Women, Energy, and *Middlemarch*." Summarizing her experience, Edwards concludes:

> Thus, like most women, I have gone through my entire education—as both student and teacher—as a schizophrenic, and I do not use this term lightly, for madness is the bizarre but logical conclusion of our education. Imagining myself male, I attempted to create myself male. Although I knew the case was otherwise, it seemed I could do nothing to make this other critically real.

Edwards extends her analysis by linking this condition to the effects of the stereotypical presentation of women in literature:

> I said simply, and for the most part silently that, since neither those women nor any women whose acquaintances I had made in fiction had much to do with the life I led or wanted to lead, I was not female. Alien from the women I saw most frequently imagined, I mentally arranged them in rows labelled respectively insipid heroines, sexy survivors, and demonic destroyers. As organizer I stood somewhere else, alone perhaps, but hopefully above them.[10]

Intellectually male, sexually female, one is in effect no one, nowhere, immasculated.

Clearly, then, the first act of the feminist critic must be to become a resisting rather than an assenting reader and, by this refusal to assent, to begin the process of exorcizing the male mind that has been implanted in us. The consequence of this exorcism is the capacity for what Adrienne Rich describes as re-vision—"the act of looking back, of seeing with fresh eyes, of entering an old text from a new critical direction." And the consequence, in turn, of this re-vision is that books will no longer be read as they have been read and thus will lose their power to bind us unknowingly to their designs. While women obviously cannot rewrite literary works so that they become ours by virtue of reflecting our reality, we can accurately name the reality they do reflect and so change literary criticism from a closed conversation to an active dialogue.

In making available to women this power of naming reality, feminist criticism is revolutionary. The significance of such power is evident if one considers the strength of the taboos against it:

I permit no woman to teach . . . she is to keep silent.
                                                    —*St. Paul*

By Talmudic law a man could divorce a wife whose voice could be heard next door. From there to Shakespeare: "Her voice was ever soft,/Gentle, and low—an excellent thing in woman." And to Yeats: "The women that I picked spoke sweet and low/ And yet gave tongue." And to Samuel Beckett, guessing at the last torture, The Worst: "a woman's voice perhaps, I hadn't thought of that, they might engage a soprano."   —*Mary Ellmann*[11]

The experience of the class in which I voiced my discontent still haunts my nightmares. Until my face froze and my brain congealed, I was called prude and, worse yet, insensitive, since I willfully misread the play in the interest of proving a point false both to the work and in itself.
                                                    —*Lee Edwards*[12]

The experience Edwards describes of attempting to communicate her reading of the character of Shakespeare's Cleopatra is a common memory for most of us who have become feminist critics. Many of us never spoke; those of us who did speak were usually quickly silenced. The need to keep certain things from being thought and said reveals to us their importance. Feminist criticism represents the discovery/recovery of a voice, a unique and uniquely powerful voice capable of canceling out those other voices, so movingly described in Sylvia Plath's *The Bell Jar,* which spoke about us and to us and at us but never for us.

III

The eight works analyzed in this book were chosen for their individual significance, their representative value, and their collective potential. They are interconnected in the ways that they comment on and illuminate each other, and they form a dramatic whole whose meaning transcends the mere sum of the parts. These eight are meant to stand for a much larger body of literature; their individual and collective designs can be found elsewhere repeatedly.

The four short stories form a unit, as do the four novels. These units are subdivided into pairs. "Rip Van Winkle" and "I Want to Know Why" are companion pieces whose focus is the fear of and resistance to growing up. The value of Anderson's story lies mainly in the light it sheds on Irving's, making explicit the fear of sexuality only implied in "Rip" and focusing attention on the strategy of deflecting hostility away from men and onto women. "The Birthmark" and "A Rose for Emily" are richly related studies of the consequences of growing up and, by implication, of the reasons for the resistance to it. In both stories sexual desire leads to death. More significantly, they are brilliant companion analyses of that sex/class hostility that is the essence of patriarchal culture and that underlies the adult identity Anderson's boy recoils from assuming. "The Birthmark" is the story of how to murder your wife and get away with it; "A Rose for Emily" is the story of how the system which allows you to murder your wife makes it possible for your wife to murder you.

Both *A Farewell to Arms* and *The Great Gatsby* are love stories; together they demonstrate the multiple uses of the mythology of romantic love in the maintenance of male power. In addition they elaborate on the function of scapegoating evident in "Rip Van Winkle" and "The Birthmark." In its more obvious connection of the themes of love and power, *The Great Gatsby* brings closer to consciousness the hostility which *A Farewell to Arms* seeks to disguise and bury. *The Bostonians* and *An American Dream* form the most unlikely and perhaps the most fascinating of the pairs. In both, the obfuscation of romantic love has been cleared away and the issue of power directly joined. James's novel describes a social reality—male power, female powerlessness—which Mailer's denies by creating a social mythology—female power, male powerlessness—that inverts that reality. Yet finally, the intention of Mailer's mythology is to maintain the reality it denies. *The Bostonians* forces the strategies of *An American Dream* into the open by its massive documentation of women's oppression, and *An American Dream* provides the political answer to *The Bostonians'* inevitability by its massive, though unintended, demonstration of the fact that women's oppression grows not out of biology but out of men's need to oppress.

The sequence of both the stories and the novels is generated by a scale of increasing complexity, increasing consciousness, and increasing "feminist" sympathy and insight. Thus, the movement of the stories is from the black and white of "Rip Van Winkle," with its postulation of good guy and villain and its formulation in terms of innocent fable, to the complexity of "A Rose for Emily," whose action forces sexual violence into consciousness and demands understanding for the erstwhile villain. The movement of the novels is similar. *A Farewell to Arms* is as simplistic and disguised and hostile as "Rip Van Winkle"; indeed, the two have many affinities, not the least of which is the similarity of their sleep-centered protagonists who believe that women are a bad dream that will go away if you just stay in bed long enough. The sympathy and complexity of consciousness in *The Bostonians* is even larger than that in "A Rose for Emily," and is exceeded only by the imagination of *An American Dream*, which is "feminist" not be design but by default. Yet the decision to end with *An American Dream* comes not simply from its position on the incremental scale. *An American Dream* is "Rip Van Winkle" one hundred and fifty years later, intensified to be sure, but *exactly the same story*. Thus, the complete trajectory of the immasculating imagination of American literature is described by the movement from "Rip Van Winkle" to *An American Dream*, and that movement is finally circular. This juxtaposition of beginning and end provides the sharpest possible exposure of that circular quality in the design of our literature, apparent in the movements within and between works, which defines its imaginative limits. Like the race horse so loved by Anderson's boy, the imagination which informs our "classic" American literature runs endlessly round a single track, unable because unwilling to get out of the race.

ONE

PALPABLE DESIGNS
Four American Short Stories

An American Dream:
"Rip Van Winkle"

Washington Irving is reported to have spent a June evening in 1818 talking with his brother-in-law about the old days in Sleepy Hollow. Melancholy of late, the writer was pleased to find himself laughing. Suddenly he got up and went to his room. By morning he had the manuscript of the first and most famous American short story, and his best single claim to a permanent reputation.[1]

The figure of Rip Van Winkle presides over the birth of the American imagination; and it is fitting that our first successful homegrown legend should memorialize, however playfully, the flight of the dreamer from the shrew—into the mountains and out of time, away from the drab duties of home and town toward the good companions and the magic keg of beer. Ever since, the typical male protagonist of our fiction has been a man on the run, harried into the forest and out to sea, down the river or into combat—anywhere to avoid "civilization," which is to say, the confrontation of a man and woman which leads to the fall to sex, marriage, and responsibility.[2]

Engendered in melancholy, released through nostalgia, and interchanged with sleep—what better place to begin

1

than with Washington Irving's "Rip Van Winkle," the story which marked the emergence of American literature at home and abroad, which began the long dream of our fiction, and which has become an inherent part of our national mythology. In writing "Rip Van Winkle," Irving adapted to the American scene, setting, and psyche the elements of a German folk tale, itself a version of a time-honored legend. In making this translation he produced a classic statement of character and theme in American literature. As Rip is a protagonist whom one will encounter again and again in the pages of our fiction, so his story presents the fantasy woven by our writers on the underside of our national consciousness, in subconscious counterpoint to the official voice of our public rhetoric.

"Rip Van Winkle" is the dreamwork of the persona created by Benjamin Franklin in his *Autobiography,* the inevitable consequence of the massive suppressions required by Franklin's code of success. The voice to which Rip gives ear is the exact opposite of the voice embodied in the *Autobiography,* with its imperatives for self-improvement and for constant and regulated activity, for a day neatly parceled out in preplanned units, goal- and future-oriented, built on a commitment to accumulation and an investment in the notion of progress. "Early to bed and early to rise makes a man healthy, wealthy and wise," cries Franklin, to which Rip responds with an infinite desire for sleep. If Franklin's *Autobiography* represents one kind of American success story, "Rip Van Winkle" represents another, for what his story records is the successful evasion of the demands and values that speak through Franklin. And if Franklin's book is a testament to how lucky it is to be an American, "Rip Van Winkle" is perhaps the first registering of a disillusionment with America as idea and fact which Mark Twain was later to articulate in the voice of another famous villager, Pudd'nhead Wilson: "It was wonderful to find America, but it would have been more wonderful to miss it."

Central in Irving's formulation of his classic American story is the role he gives to women. The German tale on which he based "Rip" has no equivalent for Dame Van Winkle; she is Irving's creation and addition. Irving's tale is distinguished from its source by his elaboration of the psychology behind the experience of protracted sleep, and this elaboration is in turn distinguished by women's involvement in it. What drives Rip away from the village and up into the mountains and what makes him a likely partaker of the sleep-inducing liquor is his wife; all the ills from which Rip seeks escape are symbolically located in the person of the offending Dame Van Winkle. Thus, an essential part of the Americanness of Irving's story is the creation of woman as villain: as obstacle to the achievement of the dream of pleasure; as mouthpiece for the values of work, responsibility, adulthood—the imperatives of Benjamin Franklin. Significantly, Irving's tale connects the image of woman with the birth of America as a nation and with the theme of growing up.

Rip is the first in a long line of American heroes as "nice guys." He is a "great favorite" and is possessed of "universal popularity." Everybody in the village loves him; children shout with joy at his appearance and not a dog will bark at him. He is kind, simple, good-natured, and meek. He is never too busy to join the children at their sports or to run errands for the women or to assist the men in their projects. Having no concerns of his own, he responds to the needs of others. In a Benjamin Franklin world, where everyone else is busy pursuing goals, Rip represents that *summum bonum*, a person with nothing to do. His popularity derives from his availability and from a concomitant self-effacement and meekness of spirit.

There is one person with whom Rip is not popular, whom he will not serve, and whose demands go unanswered; that is, of course, his wife. The source of Rip's resistance to Dame Van Winkle is not laziness, for he will fish and hunt all day, tramping through miles of forest and swamp, up hill and down. Nor is the source of his resistance a distaste for work, since he is glad to assist in the roughest toil of the community, whether husking Indian corn or building stone fences. Rather, Rip resists Dame Van Winkle because she represents what he ought to do. What Rip rejects is the belief that the end of work is the accumulation of profit; what he resists is the imperative "thou shalt make money." Inverting Franklin's pattern of increment, the saga of the poor boy who begins with only two loaves of bread and ends as one of the richest men in the city of Philadelphia, Rip refuses to touch his patrimonial estate and has let it dwindle until it is nothing more than a poor parched acre. Yet Rip's resistance is not simply to work as a way to profit; it is equally to work as a moral imperative—that which one ought to do as opposed to that which one wants to do. Rip is willing to do everything *except* what he ought to; his commitment is to pleasure and play. Like his more famous successor, Huckleberry Finn, Rip wages a subterranean and passive revolt against the superego and its imperatives.

Rip's refusal to do what he ought is in effect a refusal to be what he ought. He rejects the role of master, preferring instead to be servant; no father to his children, he is instead the playmate of others' children; his concept of political responsibility consists of listening to the contents of months-old newspapers drawled out by the village schoolmaster and commented on by the puffs from Nicholas Vedder's pipe. Although a descendant of the Van Winkles, "who figured so gallantly in the chivalrous days of Peter Stuyvesant," Rip has inherited little of the martial character of his worthy ancestors. His pleasure in hunting lies not in killing but rather in being outside, free, roaming through woods and hills at will. Indeed, his essential lack of aggression is reflected in the way he refuses the imperatives to be otherwise. Rip's idea of fighting is the passive resistance of evasion. And what he evades, of course, is conflict: the war between the sexes, the war between the colonies and the mother country. Rip rejects the conventional image of masculinity and the behavior traditionally expected of an adult male and identifies himself with characteristics and behaviors assumed to be feminine and assigned to women. Thus, the figure who "presides over the birth of the American imagination" is in effect a female-identified woman-hater. Here is a conflict whose evasion requires all of Irving's art—and gets it; for Irving is as dedicated to avoiding conflict as his hero, sinking the history of colonial conflict in the confusion of Dutch Hendrik with English Henry, converting the tombstone connotations of R.I.P. and the death wish behind it to the fantasy of endless rebirth.

Dame Van Winkle is the unsympathetic thorn in Rip's exceedingly sympathetic side. She is the embodiment of all the values he rejects, the would-be enforcer of all the imperatives he is fleeing, the spoiler of his holiday, the enemy. "Rip Van Winkle" is one of the first American books in which man, nature, and beast (who is always male too—Rip would not go into the woods with a "bitch") are sacrosanctly linked and woman is seen as the agent of civilization that seeks to repress this holy trinity. In opposition to Rip's pleasure principle, Dame Van Winkle is voluble on the subject of work and on the value of practicality. The opposition of Rip and Dame is extended to women and men in general. In the opening paragraph Irving notes that the "good wives" of the village regard the Catskills as "perfect barometers," enabling them to forecast the weather with accuracy. How marked a contrast to the web of fancy cast over these same mountains by the narrator, Diedrich Knickerbocker. Dream states, imagination and play in "Rip Van Winkle" are clearly the prerogatives of men. The fantasy figures from the dream past who play in the Catskills are all male. Rip's "perpetual club of the sages, philosophers, and other idle personages of the village" is all male too and is dedicated to the pure pleasure of sitting long afternoons in the shade and telling "endless sleepy stories about nothing."

Dame Van Winkle is linked to civilization and to the institutions which it is composed of in another way. She is connected to politics through the somewhat elaborated metaphor of "petticoat government" and to America's coming of age as a separate political entity by virtue of the similarity between her behavior and that of the politicos Rip encounters on his return to the village; their shrill and disputatious tones are the very echo of the voice of the termagant Dame. If women are bad because they are portrayed as governmental, government is bad because it is portrayed as female. It is not hard—there are lots of pointers along the way—to get from Irving's Dame to Ken Kesey's Big Nurse, who is bad because she represents a system whose illegitimacy is underscored by the fact that *she,* a woman, represents it.

In its simplest terms, the basic fantasy "Rip Van Winkle" embodies is that of being able to sleep long enough to avoid at once the American Revolution and the wife. The story imagines and enacts a successful evasion of civilization and of the imperatives of adulthood. Rip sleeps through those years when one is expected to be politically, personally, and sexually mature and thus moves from the boyhood of youth to the boyhood of an old age that promises to go on forever. In addition, he accomplishes something else: access to life in an all-male world, a world without women, the ideal American territory. Like Melville a half-century later, Irving invokes as playground a world which is perforce exclusively male—the world of men on ships exploring new territories. Rip encounters in the mountains the classic elements of American male culture: sport invested with utter seriousness; highly ritualized nonverbal communication; liquor as communion; and the mystique of male companionship. In an act of camaraderie, based on a sure and shared instinct as to the life-expectancy of termagants, the little men provide Rip with the opportunity and instrument of escape.

The experience in the mountains, however, is not simply an act of evasion, culminating in the perfect communion of males; it is equally an act of invasion, carrying out on a larger scale the pattern of Rip's "femininity" and suggesting that the secret source of his fantasy lies in a fear and envy of women. What Rip sees in the mountains is a reversal of the pattern that prevails in the village, for here it is men who invade female territory and dominate it and drive the women out. The material appended as postscript to the story gains its significance in light of this reversal. The postscript contains Indian legends, the first of which concerns the old squaw spirit who ruled the Catskills and "influenced the weather, spreading sunshine or clouds over the landscape, and sending good or bad hunting seasons." Rip's vision in the mountains displaces this legend, making men the gods of weather and relegating women to the position of mere interpreters of their thunder. "Rip Van Winkle" constitutes a patriarchal revolution in miniature in which men assume the powers previously accorded to women and female-centered myths are replaced by male-centered myths. Emblematic of this displacement, the legend of the old squaw spirit is appended as postscript, while the epigraph of the story is an invocation to Woden, God of Saxons, whose son and sometimes other self was Thor, god of thunder.

When Rip awakens from his sleep in the mountains, his first concern is his wife—what excuse can he make to her for his "overnight" absence from home. This concern, however, soon gives way to a larger sense of unease. His clean, well-oiled gun has been replaced by a rusty old firelock with a worm-eaten stock; his dog is nowhere to be found; there is no sign anywhere of the men he encountered in the mountains or of the place where they played. Metaphorically as well as literally Rip, upon awakening, is out of joint. Unease moves toward terror as Rip returns to the village and it becomes clearer and clearer to him that the world he left is not the world he has returned to. Like the Catskills, with which he has such an affinity, Rip seems "dismembered," something left behind on a great drive forward, onward, westward. With each succeeding encounter his sense of himself becomes more and more confused until at last, when forced to identify himself, he can only cry, "I'm not myself—I'm somebody else—that's me yonder—no—that's somebody else got into my shoes—I was myself last night, but I fell asleep on the mountain, and they've changed my gun, and everything's changed, and I'm changed, and I can't tell what's my name, or who I am."

"Rip Van Winkle" is a fantasy tinged with terror, a dreamwork with hints of nightmare. Yet its tone is finally one of reconciliation and incorporation. In "Rip Van Winkle" one can go home again. Rip's village eventually believes his statement that he means no harm, dismisses its view of him as lunatic or spy, and accords him the identity of returning hero. He is embraced as one who is connected by his age to what is now perceived as that more pleasant past before the Revolution and by his experience in the mountains to that still more pleasant past before America ever was, to that time when it was still an idea in the mind of Europe. He is the one who has rejected the identities handed to him, the "perfumes" of "houses and rooms" which Whitman resists at the opening of "Song of Myself"; who has experienced the fears attendant upon such a rejection, and who has nevertheless emerged as living proof that it can be done. He has indulged the communal dream of escape from all forms of responsibility and all the forces which threaten the life of pleasure. Having slept through those years when adulthood is expected, he is allowed to remain now and forever a boy. Perceiving as he does that all that has happened in his absence is the exchange of one George for another, Rip inevitably suggests that the most meaningful relationship one can have to the Revolution is to have slept through it. His experience in the mountains at once displaces the events of the Revolution and presents itself as the logical substitute for them. The real act of rebellion in Irving's tale is Rip's, and it is he who has enacted the real American Revolution. Thus, it is proper that he is recognized by the little men as one fit to join that long line of heroes who have disappeared into mountains where they sleep and wait until their time and world is ready.[3]

But what is a woman to do with "Rip Van Winkle"? How is she to read our "first and most famous" story in which the American imagination is born if the defining act of that imagination is to identify the real American Revolution with the avoidance of adulthood, which means the avoidance of women, which means the avoidance of one's wife? What is the impact of this American dream on her? The answer is obvious: disastrous. What is an essentially simple act of identification when the reader of the story is male becomes a tangle of contradictions when the reader is female. Where in this story is the female reader to locate herself? Certainly she is not Rip, for the fantasy he embodies is thoroughly male and is defined precisely by its opposition to woman. Nor is she Dame Van Winkle, for Dame is not a person: she is a scapegoat, the enemy, the OTHER. Without name or identity other than that of Rip's Dame, she is summarized, explained, and dismissed through the convention of stereotypes as a "termagant wife," a shrew, a virago. Because she is abstracted and reduced to a stereotype whose mechanism she endlessly repeats, her death is presented as a joke on that mechanism and is viewed as a great relief. Dame Van Winkle is a male mechanism, not a woman. What, then, of her daughter, Judith, who takes Rip in where Dame threw him out and who appears to be a pleasant alternative to her mother? Yet, what is Judith really except her mother married to someone other than her father? Marry her to her brother and, sure enough, you would have a daughter as like the mother as the son is like the father.

The woman who reads "Rip Van Winkle" finds herself excluded from the experience of the story. She is no part of the act of resistance, nor does she recognize herself in that which is being resisted. Indeed, the full extent of her exclusion can be seen in the fact that those qualitites which are potentially admirable aspects of the female role are assigned to Rip and made positive because they are part of *his* character, while what is negative about the male role is accorded to Dame Van Winkle, who is made a masculine authority figure and damned for it.

It would be nice if the female reader, upon realizing the dimensions of her exclusion from the story, could dismiss "Rip Van Winkle" as having nothing to do with her. Unfortunately, however, the story enforces a certain experience on her. While not identifying with Dame Van Winkle, she nevertheless cannot fully escape the sense of being somehow implicated in the indictment of her sex that Dame Van Winkle represents. She cannot read the story without being assaulted by the negative images of women it presents. Primary among them is that view, as pervasive in American literature as it is in Western culture, of women as each other's natural and instinctive enemies: "Certain it is that he was a great favorite among the good wives of the village, who, as usual with the amiable sex, took his part in all family squabbles and never failed, whenever they talked those matters over in their evening gossipings, to lay all the blame on Dame Van Winkle." Surely this is one of Irving's nastier ironies, an example of what Philip Young calls his "whimsical antifeminism."[4] And the real rub is the fact that the story forces the female reader to enact its definition of her sex. A woman reading "Rip Van Winkle" becomes perforce one of Irving's "good wives," taking Rip's side and laying all the blame on Dame Van Winkle; that is the way the story is written. The consequence for the female reader is a divided self. She is asked to identify with Rip and against herself, to scorn the amiable sex and act just like it, to laugh at Dame Van Winkle and accept that she represents "woman," to be at once both repressor and repressed, and ultimately to realize that she is neither. Rip's words upon returning home after his twenty-year evasion are ironically appropriate to her: "I'm not myself—I'm somebody else—that's me yonder—no—that's somebody else . . . I can't tell what's my name, or who I am."

The somewhat ironic tone Irving adopts toward his material might be adduced as evidence of a certain complexity to his immasculating imagination. He puts the story in the mouth of Diedrich Knickerbocker, who has already been established as a figure of fun in *Knickerbocker's History of New York*. The frame of the story makes us aware that there is more than one teller of this tale, and we would be wrong to miss the ironic Irving behind the dreamy Knickerbocker. The difficulty, however, is that Irving's irony seems finally a gesture, a sop thrown to the critical faculties of his readers so that he may the more successfully float his fantasy. Irving is still committed to his dream and to the antifeminism underlying it, despite the fact that he casts it as a joke. For however much he may mock Rip and protest that his tale is but a fantasy, Dame Van Winkle is still stuck with the stigmata of her shrewhood and the effect of Irving's story is still to make escaping her a national good, an American dream.

Growing Up Male in America:
"I Want to Know Why"

Sherwood Anderson's "I Want to Know Why" is Rip Van Winkle's dream turned nightmare, for what Irving avoids Anderson confronts. What is implicit in Irving's tale, what he displaces to the postscript whose legends tell of the "bewildered hunter" left "aghast on the brink of a beetling precipice or raging torrent," is in Anderson's story explicit and central. The fantasy of the successful evasion of adulthood becomes the nightmare of being unable to grow up, and this failure is clearly linked to a vision of what it means to be male, which is in turn linked to a fear of sexuality. The nightmare quality of Anderson's story is the result of its making these connections; the sunny tone of Irving's tale is purchased by its evasion of them. Remove the structure of fantasy that supports "Rip Van Winkle," replace those elements which Irving has evaded and displaced, and the result is "I Want to Know Why": a story about a boy who loves horses and stables and tracks and the various males who associate with them; who cuts out for Saratoga to watch his favorite horse and favorite man in action; who later follows this favorite man to a little farmhouse away from the tracks and through a window watches him kissing a whore; who is totally shattered by this experience and at the end can only reiterate a question for which he knows there are no answers.

The fear of sexuality that is an obvious source of the boy's trauma in "I Want to Know Why" is implicit in "Rip Van Winkle." One can't avoid the symbolic overtones of Irving's landscape[5] or the suggestion that on one level Rip's flight from Dame Van Winkle is a flight from sexuality. Nevertheless, fear of sexuality remains in "Rip Van

Winkle" a very heavily obscured and minor motif, an implication only. Dame Van Winkle hardly appears as a sexual force—indeed, Rip's children are difficult to account for; it would seem more likely that he sprung them magically from some part of himself in order to have playmates—and Rip's resistance to growing up is focused elsewhere than on sexuality.

The evasion of sexuality is, however, symptomatic of a larger evasion. The crisis of identity that Rip experiences on coming down from the mountains is diminished by the villagers' rather ready extension of an identity to him. But that crisis and its terror are real enough; they are the inevitable consequence of Rip's overt rejection of the masculine role expected of him and his implicit adoption of the potentially degrading female role. What permits Irving to avoid the implications of his fantasy is, of course, the figure of Dame Van Winkle. By casting Dame Van Winkle in the role of civilizing agent, Irving is able to disguise the conflict at the heart of his hero's character and to deflect hostility away from its actual object. For if the imperative to grow up comes from a woman, then resistance to that imperative need not be seen as feminine and Rip's reluctance to be masculine can be safely concealed. If woman can be made to play the masculine role, then she can be made a scapegoat, and it is possible to displace onto her the anger toward men that is the real issue. This strategy is a safe one because it originates in the perception that women have no real power and cannot strike back if attacked. It is the safety of this strategy, in combination with its dishonesty, that makes the termagant wife one of the great American jokes. At some level, men's cowering before their wives always partakes of the element of pose and the posture of the mock-heroic. America's greatest humorist, Mark Twain, creates his wife Livy in the image of a termagant and shares it with his male friends as a consciously created joke. The same tone underlies the scene in which Rip and Wolf cower before the broom of Dame Van Winkle. Anderson, however, does not rely on the easy strategy of the scapegoat, and "I Want to Know Why" is hardly comic. What Anderson's boy resists is not just growing up; it is specifically growing up *male*.* His anger is clearly directed against men, and his realization of this hostility is the story's central trauma.

The narrator of "I Want to Know Why" sees the world in terms of two clearly differentiated categories: boys, which by definition includes "niggers," and men. These categories permeate his consciousness; he never mentions a boy without saying what his father does. He is obsessed by the question of what men do and are because he wants to know what he will do and be. The central action of the story is the boy's search for an acceptable adult male role model, and the failure of the trainer, Jerry Tillford, to provide such a model forms the climax of the story, leaving the boy stranded in a limbo world: he can't go home again because he has ceased to be a boy, but neither can he go on because the vision of manhood offered to him is intolerable. The trip the boy takes to Saratoga is a metaphor for his search for an adult identity, and it ends, as does the parallel journey from the Saratoga tracks to the "little rummy-looking farm house set in a yard," with the wish that "I hadn't gone away from the tracks, but had stayed with the boys and the niggers and the horses," with the wish that one could be like Rip Van Winkle and stay forever in the world of boys, that one never had to grow up.

A chasm exists between the world the boy lives in and the world that men inhabit. Their world is distant from

*It is worth noting that Anderson's story is not the only American work to explore this theme. For example, Melville, through such figures as Ahab and Captain Vere, is concerned to trace the consequences of excessive masculinity. In the image of Ahab, impaled on the bone which he has cut from the phallic whale and used as a surrogate limb, Melville makes an explicit statement of these consequences.

his: "The men from home stayed mostly in the grandstand and betting field, and didn't come out around the places where the horses are kept except to the paddocks just before a race when the horses are saddled." They are essentially absent. They are always moving about, "going over to Lexington or to the spring meeting at Churchill Downs or to Latonia." They only "come home to spend a week before they start out again." And though they follow the horses, they aren't really with them, unlike the boys and niggers who live in the stables and eat and sleep with the horses. Further, the owners of many of the horses are literally absentee landlords; they own farms in Kentucky but live in New York. Absence permeates the boy's relation to his father. Though his father is physically at home, he is no more present for his son than the horsemen fathers who are forever on the move. He refuses to relate to his son: he doesn't whip the boy for eating his cigar; when the boy returns home from Saratoga, he doesn't say much; when the boy's mother tries to prevent his going to the tracks in the morning, the father tells her, in a phrase which summarizes his relationship to his son, "Let him alone." In contrast to Henry Rieback's father, who "is always sending Henry presents," the boy's father "don't make much money and can't buy me things." But, of course, things are not that important to the boy, and the contrast he draws between Henry Rieback's father and his own is his attempt to express a larger and less tangible disappointment. It is clear that the father shares none of his son's enthusiasm for horses and evidently feels no need to try. And it is equally clear that the boy expects no real information or understanding from his father, because, significantly, he does not go to his father for help in sorting out his experience at Saratoga. The father confines himself to not interfering with his son's development, to leaving him free to discover for himself his own identity. But the implication of the story is that such a role is insufficient. It is impossible for the boy to realize himself in the absence of adult models for that self. In this critical area his father is as absent as all the other men in the boy's world.

The journey to Saratoga can be seen, then, as the boy's attempt to bridge the gap between the two worlds of boys and men. The journey is an act of imitation: "We fixed it all up and laid low until the Kentucky spring meetings were over and some of our men, the sportiest ones, the ones we envied the most, had cut out—then we cut out too." This process is made difficult, however, by the complexity of the boy's attitude toward the men he wishes to imitate. On the one hand he admires them, on the other he fears and distrusts them. When the boys arrive in Saratoga they don't go to men for help but to niggers, who are "all right about things like that," who "won't squeal on you." White men are not "all right": "Often a white man you might meet, when you had run away from home like that, might appear to be all right and give you a quarter or a half dollar or something, and then go right and give you away." Niggers and boys are trustworthy, "square"; men are treacherous and deceitful. Harry Hellinfinger, who is "grown up," tells the boy that if he eats half a cigar it will stunt his growth so that maybe he can be a rider; Jerry Tillford becomes just like other men when he pretends to a mystic communion with the boy and then betrays the experience by looking at a whore the same way he looked at the horse Sunstreak.

Another characteristic of the white adult male world is that the things men say don't make sense. The real sources of knowledge in the story are boys, niggers, and old men. It is niggers like Bildad who know how to get what they want. It is boys like the narrator who know the fact, if not the reasons for it, that niggers are square and white men aren't. It is boys and niggers and old men who can assess the qualities of Middlestride and Sunstreak—"we had never sent a pair like that to the races before. Old men in

Beckersville said so and the niggers said so. It was a fact"—and can pick out a winner among the new colts. In contrast, the men are characterized by assertion without reason. Under the guise of authority, they present the boy with a series of riddles and no clues: "That's all right and I guess the men know what they are talking about, but I don't see what it's got to do with Henry or horses either." The boy is not questioning here the men's assessment of gambling as something bad, nor is he questioning their assertion that gambling and horses share the same world. The riddle for him is rather the implication that there is some *necessary* connection between these things; that because Henry's father is a gambler Henry must necessarily be affected; that because men gamble on horses one's attitude toward horses must be changed. What the boy resists is the implication that good and evil cannot coexist without intermingling, that if one is exposed to evil one will inevitably "embrace" it. In the way men think, the boy senses the potential for spoiling his world and contaminating his mind.

Given this vision, it is no wonder the boy is ambivalent on the subject of growing up. If he has conceived his journey to Saratoga in imitation of the men he envies, he has also shown considerable resistance to thinking of himself as a man. Initially he has tried to stunt his growth in order to be a rider, who, in his terminology, is still a boy. Then he has dreamed of being a stable boy, but only niggers do that. Only reluctantly has he come to accept his destiny: "I am always wanting to be a trainer or owner." It is with Jerry Tillford that the boy for the first time feels positive about this destiny, for in Jerry he feels he has found an adult role model, someone whom he can respect and with whom he can identify. In contrast to the distancing that characterizes his view of adult men throughout the story, the experience in the paddock is characterized by a physical contact that encloses boy, horse, and man in a magical circle of perfect understanding. Because the boy sees in Jerry a man who shares *his* passions and values, the world of boys and the world of men touch and for the first time there is a possibility of continuity between the two. The boy can project himself into adulthood without having to imagine some radical change in his nature. For the first time he can talk specifically about what an adult does and he can imagine himself doing it. The crucial nature of the boy's experience is indicated by the fact that he finds himself thinking more about the man than about the horse and that after the race he wants to "cut out from Tom and Hanley and Henry" to be by himself and if possible near Jerry; he wants to dissociate himself from the boys and solidify his newly found adult identification.

But Jerry turns out to be just like all the other men the boy has known, except that this time the knowledge is disastrous; after it nothing is ever again the same: "At the tracks the air don't taste as good or smell as good." In proving conclusively that men are everything the boy has thought them to be, Jerry presents an intolerable vision of what it means to grow up and cuts off the boy's last hope of escaping this destiny. At the same time, the boy's experience with Jerry has begun the very process he fears. Having once identified with Jerry, the boy can never again be just a boy; having once allowed the boy's world and the man's world to make contact, the boy can never again be safely insulated in his world. He can no more go backward than he can go forward. This boy, in spite of his ardent wish, is not going to be "O.K."

Because the moment of illumination and horror occurs for the boy when he discovers Jerry kissing a whore, it is reasonable to assume that attitudes toward sexuality and, concomitantly, attitudes toward women play a large part in the boy's revulsion at the thought of growing up. We might, therefore, gain some further insight into why the experience with Jerry is so disastrous for the boy if we examine the attitude toward women implicit in the story. As in "Rip Van Winkle," the ideal world in Sherwood Anderson's story is a world without women. The narrator lives in a totally male environment—boys, men, niggers, even the horses are male—and this is the way he wants it to be and the way he wants to keep it. Women appear only twice in the story and both times negatively. The mother is a stereotypical figure of contempt: "Mother wouldn't of let me go"; "Mother jawed and cried." Just as in "Rip Van Winkle," the positive elements of the female role are co-opted by men. It is niggers who cook so as to make your mouth water and it is niggers who find you a place to sleep and provide the warmth and security of a home. And it is Jerry who is the approving mother: "I knew that for him it was like a mother seeing her child do something brave or wonderful." Similarly, the image of woman is positive only when defined as impossible fantasy: Sunstreak is "like a girl you think about sometimes but never see." The only good woman is an idea in one's head; she doesn't exist. Real women, the women that one sees, are not at all like "a girl you think about"; they are whores in a rummy farmhouse—ugly, hard, mean, and dirty; objects of horror, disgust, fear. And consequently, adult sexuality is perceived as nightmare. If growing up means sex and if sex means *them*, then no wonder the boy is distraught. In horror and rage he recoils from this traumatic vision of the self as adult, "so mad clean through that I cried and my fists were doubled up so my fingernails cut my hand."

The boy's rage, however, is clearly directed against the men, not against the whores, because he realizes that, while the women may be disgusting, the men's relation to them is more so. Throughout the story the boy has resisted the exploitative relationship to things and people that he feels is characteristic of men, the kind of relationship that is expressed through the metaphor of gambling. Men relate to horses for profit, not for love; they *use* horses. The boy knows he has the potential for this kind of relationship—he could be a gambler if he wished. But he doesn't so wish and he thinks that in Jerry he has found a man who shares his values. However, what he witnesses at the farmhouse reveals that Jerry is just as exploitative as other men. Jerry uses Sunstreak; he takes credit for the horse's accomplishments in order to glorify himself in the eyes of the other men and the whores. Jerry also uses women. In perceiving that the relationship of men to women is exploitative, the boy makes a connection between the way men treat women and the way they treat boys like himself. Whether the men give the boys money and betray them, or the whores money and use them sexually the attitude is the same: contemptuous, patronizing, and possessive. In both cases the relation is commercial; money is used in place of love. The boy not only identifies Jerry's whore with the horse; he identifies her with himself. Women, horses, children—they are all objects of exploitation by men. And it is precisely here that we come upon the full horror of the boy's situation, for what his experience has shown him is that when he grows up his relation to women will inevitably duplicate the men's relation to him. The power of the story derives from the defeat of the boy's desire to avoid becoming his father. By the end of the story, the boy has realized that there is no continuity between the world of boyhood and the world of adulthood and that the physical distance which separates them is but a metaphor for psychic territory that can be crossed only at the cost of a radical transformation of the self.

The end of "I Want to Know Why" presents the classic situation of the American protagonist: abandoned in a paradise gone bad. And, as is the case with so much American literature, it is clear that all that art can do is record the horror. It cannot provide an answer, a solution, or a compensation. At best it can allow a temporary return to the lost world of boyhood; at most it can delay the moment of confrontation which will destroy that innocence. And delay the narrator does, compulsively: "Well, I must tell you"; "That's what I'm writing about"; "Here it is"; "I'll tell you about that"; "Here is what happened." Yet, if in telling the story the boy temporarily regains his lost world, nevertheless the story only exists because that world *has* been lost and so, inevitably, it moves toward the horrified realization. But all the story can do is express the horror; it cannot resolve it. Indeed, the limitations of art are defined by the very form of the question the boy asks, which, like his life and his story, can go nowhere. The narrator of "I Want to Know Why" has no escape except to tell a story that exists only because of a horror it cannot resolve, ameliorate, or transcend. Like the racehorse he admires, the boy is locked in a circular track, beginning only to end in order to begin again.

There is a feminist dimension to Anderson's story. The boy's resistance to growing up is clearly defined as a reluctance to grow up *male,* and the source of this reluctance is linked to his culture's attitudes toward women. Yet, finally, to express the consequences for men of their patriarchal system is of limited value for women. The woman reader is still faced with a story whose concern is entirely for men and their dilemmas, a story in which what happens to women is of no importance at all. And this exclusion is particularly annoying when one realizes that the situation of Anderson's protagonist is analogous to the situation of the woman reading "Rip Van Winkle." Lack of acceptable identity is the traumatic factor in both cases and namelessness, self-hatred, and limbo are the consequences. Yet such phenomena are more readily legitimized as the subject matter for art and consciousness when the divided self is male. Readers who smile knowingly at Irving's analysis of the "amiable" sex and who would dismiss as trivial, if not

imaginary, the conflicts experienced by women in reading
his story may well leave Anderson's story with an acute
sense of pain at the "universal" tragedy it embodies and
with an immense sympathy for the difficulties boys experience in trying to be men.

Women Beware Science:
"The Birthmark"

The scientist Aylmer in Nathaniel Hawthorne's "The
Birthmark" provides another stage in the psychological
history of the American protagonist. Aylmer is Irving's
Rip and Anderson's boy discovered in that middle age
which Rip evades and the boy rejects. Aylmer is squarely
confronted with the realities of marriage, sex, and women.
There are compensations, however, for as an adult he has
access to a complex set of mechanisms for accomplishing
the great American dream of eliminating women. It is testimony at once to Hawthorne's ambivalence, his seeking to
cover with one hand what he uncovers with the other, and
to the pervasive sexism of our culture that most readers
would describe "The Birthmark" as a story of failure
rather than as the success story it really is—the demonstration of how to murder your wife and get away with it.
It is, of course, possible to read "The Birthmark" as a story
of misguided idealism, a tale of the unhappy consequences
of man's nevertheless worthy passion for perfecting and
transcending nature; and this is the reading usually given
it.[6] This reading, however, ignores the significance of the
form idealism takes in the story. It is not irrelevant that
"The Birthmark" is about a man's desire to perfect his
wife, nor is it accidental that the consequence of this
idealism is the wife's death. In fact, "The Birthmark" provides a brilliant analysis of the sexual politics of idealiza-

tion and a brilliant exposure of the mechanisms whereby
hatred can be disguised as love, neurosis can be disguised
as science, murder can be disguised as idealization, and
success can be disguised as failure. Thus, Hawthorne's insistence in his story on the metaphor of disguise serves as
both warning and clue to a feminist reading.

Even a brief outline is suggestive. A man, dedicated to
the pursuit of science, puts aside his passion in order to
marry a beautiful woman. Shortly after the marriage he
discovers that he is deeply troubled by a tiny birthmark on
her left cheek. Of negligible importance to him before
marriage, the birthmark now assumes the proportions of
an obsession. He reads it as a sign of the inevitable imperfection of all things in nature and sees in it a challenge to
man's ability to transcend nature. So nearly perfect as she
is, he would have her be completely perfect. In pursuit of
this lofty aim, he secludes her in chambers that he has
converted for the purpose, subjects her to a series of
influences, and finally presents her with a potion which, as
she drinks it, removes at last the hated birthmark but kills
her in the process. At the end of the story Georgiana is
both perfect and dead.

One cannot imagine this story in reverse—that is, a
woman's discovering an obsessive need to perfect her
husband and deciding to perform experiments on him—
nor can one imagine the story being about a man's conceiving such an obsession for another man. It is woman, and
specifically woman as wife, who elicits the obsession with
imperfection and the compulsion to achieve perfection,
just as it is man, and specifically man as husband, who is
thus obsessed and compelled. In addition, it is clear from
the summary that the imagined perfection is purely physical. Aylmer is not concerned with the quality of Georgiana's character or with the state of her soul, for he considers her "fit for heaven without tasting death." Rather,
he is absorbed in her physical appearance, and perfection

for him is equivalent to physical beauty. Georgiana is an exemplum of woman as beautiful object, reduced to and defined by her body. And finally, the conjunction of perfection and nonexistence, while reminding us of Anderson's story in which the good girl is the one you never see, develops what is only implicit in that story: namely, that the only good woman is a dead one and that the motive underlying the desire to perfect is the need to eliminate. "The Birthmark" demonstrates the fact that the idealization of women has its source in a profound hostility toward women and that it is at once a disguise for this hostility and the fullest expression of it.

The emotion that generates the drama of "The Birthmark" is revulsion. Aylmer is moved not by the vision of Georgiana's potential perfection but by his horror at her present condition. His revulsion for the birthmark is insistent: he can't bear to see it or touch it; he has nightmares about it; he has to get it out. Until she is "fixed," he can hardly bear the sight of her and must hide her away in secluded chambers which he visits only intermittently, so great is his fear of contamination. Aylmer's compulsion to perfect Georgiana is a result of his horrified perception of what she actually is, and all his lofty talk about wanting her to be perfect so that just this once the potential of Nature will be fulfilled is but a cover for his central emotion of revulsion. But Aylmer is a creature of disguise and illusion. In order to persuade this beautiful woman to become his wife, he "left his laboratory to the care of an assistant, cleared his fine countenance from the furnace smoke, washed the stains of acid from his fingers." Best not to let her know who he really is or what he really feels, lest she might say before the marriage instead of after, "You cannot love what shocks you!" In the chambers where Aylmer secludes Georgiana, "airy figures, absolutely bodiless ideas, and forms of unsubstantial beauty" come disguised as substance in an illusion so nearly perfect as to "warrant the belief that her husband possessed sway over the spiritual world." While Aylmer does not really possess sway over the spiritual world, he certainly controls Georgiana and he does so in great part because of his mastery of the art of illusion.

If the motive force for Aylmer's action in the story is repulsion, it is the birthmark that is the symbolic location of all that repels him. And it is important that the birthmark is just that: a birth *mark,* that is, something physical; and a *birth* mark, that is, something not acquired but inherent, one of Georgiana's givens, in fact equivalent to her.[7] The close connection between Georgiana and her birthmark is continually emphasized. As her emotions change, so does the birthmark, fading or deepening in response to her feelings and providing a precise clue to her state of mind. Similarly, when her senses are aroused, stroked by the influences that pervade her chamber, the birthmark throbs sympathetically. In his efforts to get rid of the birthmark Aylmer has "administered agents powerful enough to do aught except change your entire physical system," and these have failed. The object of Aylmer's obsessive revulsion, then, is Georgiana's "physical system," and what defines this particular system is the fact that it is female. It is Georgiana's female physiology, which is to say her sexuality, that is the object of Aylmer's relentless attack. The link between Georgiana's birthmark and her sexuality is implicit in the birthmark's role as her emotional barometer, but one specific characteristic of the birthmark makes the connection explicit: the hand which shaped Georgiana's birth has left its mark on her in *blood.* The birthmark is redolent with references to the particular nature of female sexuality; we hardly need Aylmer's insistence on seclusion, with its reminiscences of the treatment of women when they are "unclean," to point us in this direction. What repels Aylmer is Georgiana's sexuality; what is imperfect in her is the fact that she is female; and what perfection means is elimination.

In Hawthorne's analysis the idealization of women stems

from a vision of them as hideous and unnatural; it is a form of compensation, an attempt to bring them up to the level of nature. To symbolize female physiology as a blemish, a deformity, a birthmark suggests that women are in need of some such redemption. Indeed, "The Birthmark" is a parable of woman's relation to the cult of female beauty, a cult whose political function is to remind women that they are, in their natural state, unacceptable, imperfect, monstrous. Una Stannard in "The Mask of Beauty" has done a brilliant job of analyzing the implications of this cult:

> Every day, in every way, the billion-dollar beauty business tells women they are monsters in disguise. Every ad for bras tells a woman that her breasts need lifting, every ad for padded bras that what she's got isn't big enough, every ad for girdles that her belly sags and her hips are too wide, every ad for high heels that her legs need propping, every ad for cosmetics that her skin is too dry, too oily, too pale, or too ruddy, or her lips are not bright enough, or her lashes not long enough, every ad for deodorants and perfumes that her natural odors all need disguising, every ad for hair dye, curlers, and permanents that the hair she was born with is the wrong color or too straight or too curly, and lately ads for wigs tell her that she would be better off covering up nature's mistake completely. In this culture women are told they are the fair sex, but at the same time that their "beauty" needs lifting, shaping, dyeing, painting, curling, padding. Women are really being told that "the beauty" is a beast.[8]

The dynamics of idealization are beautifully contained in an analogy which Hawthorne, in typical fashion, remarks on casually: "But it would be as reasonable to say that one of those small blue stains which sometimes occur in the purest statuary marble would convert the Eve of Powers to a monster." This comparison, despite its apparent protest against just such a conclusion, implies that

where women are concerned it doesn't take much to convert purity into monstrosity; Eve herself is a classic example of the ease with which such a transition can occur. And
the transition is easy because the presentation of woman's
image in marble is essentially an attempt to disguise and
cover a monstrous reality. Thus, the slightest flaw will have
an immense effect, for it serves as a reminder of the reality
that produces the continual need to cast Eve in the form of
purest marble and women in the molds of idealization.

In exploring the sources of men's compulsion to idealize
women Hawthorne is writing a story about the sickness of
men, not a story about the flawed and imperfect nature of
women. There is a hint of the nature of Aylmer's ailment
in the description of his relation to "mother" Nature, a
suggestion that his revulsion for Georgiana has its root in
part in a jealousy of the power which her sexuality represents and a frustration in the face of its inpenetrable mystery. Aylmer's scientific aspirations have as their ultimate
goal the desire to create human life, but "the latter pursuit,
however, Aylmer had long laid aside in unwilling recognition of the truth—against which all seekers sooner or later
stumble—that our great creative Mother, while she amuses
us with apparently working in the broadest sunshine, is yet
severely careful to keep her own secrets, and, in spite of
her pretended openness, shows us nothing but results. She
permits us, indeed, to mar, but seldom to mend, and, like a
jealous patentee, on no account to make." This passage is
striking for its undercurrent of jealousy, hostility, and
frustration toward a specifically female force. In the vision
of Nature as playing with man, deluding him into thinking
he can acquire her power, and then at the last minute
closing him off and allowing him only the role of one who
mars, Hawthorne provides another version of woman as
enemy, the force that interposes between man and the
accomplishment of his deepest desires. Yet Hawthorne lo-

cates the source of this attitude in man's jealousy of
woman's having something he does not and his rage at
being excluded from participating in it.

Out of Aylmer's jealousy at feeling less than Nature and
thus less than woman—for if Nature is woman, woman is
also Nature and has, by virtue of her biology, a power he
does not—comes his obsessional program for perfecting
Georgiana. Believing he is less, he has to convince himself
he is more: "and then, most beloved, what will be my
triumph when I shall have corrected what Nature left imperfect in her fairest work! Even Pygmalion, when his
sculptured woman assumed life, felt not greater ecstasy
than mine will be." What a triumph indeed to upstage and
outdo Nature and make himself superior to her. The
function of the fantasy that underlies the myth of Pygmalion, as it underlies the myth of Genesis (making Adam, in
the words of Mary Daly, "the first among history's unmar-
ried pregnant males"[9]), is obvious from the reality which it
seeks to invert. Such myths are powerful image builders,
salving man's injured ego by convincing him that he is not
only equal to but better than woman, for he creates in spite
of, against, and finally better than nature. Yet Aylmer's
failure here is as certain as the failure of his other "experiments," for the sickness which he carries within him makes
him able only to destroy, not to create.

If Georgiana is envied and hated because she represents
what is different from Aylmer and reminds him of what he
is not and cannot be, she is feared for her similarity to him
and for the fact that she represents aspects of himself that
he finds intolerable. Georgiana is as much a reminder to
Aylmer of what he is as of what he is not. This apparently
contradictory pattern of double-duty is understandable in
the light of feminist analyses of female characters in literature, who frequently function this way. Mirrors for men,
they serve to indicate the involutions of the male psyche
with which literature is primarily concerned, and their

characters and identities shift accordingly. They are pro-
jections, not people; and thus coherence of characterization is a concept that often makes sense only when applied
to the male characters of a particular work. Hawthorne's
tale is a classic example of the woman as mirror, for, despite Aylmer's belief that his response to Georgiana is an
objective concern for the intellectual and spiritual problem
she presents, it is obvious that his reaction to her is intensely subjective. "Shocks you, my husband?" queries
Georgiana, thus neatly exposing his mask, for one is not
shocked by objective perceptions. Indeed, Aylmer views
Georgiana's existence as a personal insult and threat to
him, which, of course, it is, because what he sees in her is
that part of himself he cannot tolerate. By the desire she
elicits in him to marry her and possess her birthmark, she
forces him to confront his own earthiness and "imperfection."

But it is precisely to avoid such a confrontation that
Aylmer has fled to the kingdom of science, where he can
project himself as a "type of the spiritual element." Unlike
Georgiana, in whom the physical and the spiritual are
complexly intertwined, Aylmer is hopelessly alienated
from himself. Through the figure of Aminadab, the
shaggy creature of clay, Hawthorne presents sharply the
image of Aylmer's alienation. Aminadab symbolizes that
earthly, physical, erotic self that has been split off from
Aylmer, that he refuses to recognize as part of himself,
and that has become monstrous and grotesque as a result:
"With his vast strength, his shaggy hair, his smoky aspect,
and the indescribable earthiness that incrusted him, he
seemed to represent man's physical nature; while Aylmer's
slender figure, and pale, intellectual face, were no less apt
a type of the spiritual element." Aminadab's allegorical
function is obvious and so is his connection to Aylmer, for
while Aylmer may project himself as objective, intellectual,
and scientific and while he may pretend to be totally unre-

lated to the creature whom he keeps locked up in his dark room to do his dirty work, he cannot function without him. It is Aminadab, after all, who fires the furnace for Aylmer's experiments; physicality provides the energy for Aylmer's "science" just as revulsion generates his investment in idealization. Aylmer is, despite his pretenses to the contrary, a highly emotional man: his scientific interests tend suspiciously toward fires and volcanoes; he is given to intense emotional outbursts; and his obsession with his wife's birthmark is a feeling so profound as to disrupt his entire life. Unable to accept himself for what he is, Aylmer constructs a mythology of science and adopts the character of a scientist to disguise his true nature and to hide his real motives, from himself as well as others. As a consequence, he acquires a way of acting out these motives without in fact having to be aware of them. One might describe "The Birthmark" as an exposé of science because it demonstrates the ease with which science can be invoked to conceal highly subjective motives. "The Birthmark" is an exposure of the realities that underlie the scientist's posture of objectivity and rationality and the claims of science to operate in an amoral and value-free world. Pale Aylmer, the intellectual scientist, is a mask for the brutish, earthy, soot-smeared Aminadab, just as the mythology of scientific research and objectivity finally masks murder, disguising Georgiana's death as just one more experiment that failed.

Hawthorne's attitude toward men and their fantasies is more critical than either Irving's or Anderson's. One responds to Aylmer not with pity but with horror. For, unlike Irving and Anderson, Hawthorne has not omitted from his treatment of men an image of the consequences of their ailments for the women who are involved with them. The result of Aylmer's massive self-deception is to live in an unreal world, a world filled with illusions, semblances, and appearances, one which admits of no sunlight and makes no contact with anything outside itself and at whose center is a laboratory, the physical correlative of his utter solipsism. Nevertheless, Hawthorne makes it clear that Aylmer has got someone locked up in that laboratory with him. While "The Birthmark" is by no means explicitly feminist, since Hawthorne seems as eager to be misread and to conceal as he is to be read and to reveal, still it is impossible to read his story without being aware that Georgiana is completely in Aylmer's power. For the subject is finally power. Aylmer is able to project himself onto Georgiana and to work out his obsession through her because as woman and as wife she is his possession and in his power; and because as man he has access to the language and structures of that science which provides the mechanisms for such a process and legitimizes it. In addition, since the power of definition and the authority to make those definitions stick is vested in men, Aylmer can endow his illusions with the weight of spiritual aspiration and universal truth.

The implicit feminism in "The Birthmark" is considerable. On one level the story is a study of sexual politics, of the powerlessness of women and of the psychology which results from that powerlessness. Hawthorne dramatizes the fact that woman's identity is a product of men's responses to her: "It must not be concealed, however, that the impression wrought by this fairy sign manual varied exceedingly, according to the difference of temperament in the beholders." To those who love Georgiana, her birthmark is evidence of her beauty; to those who envy or hate her, it is an object of disgust. It is Aylmer's repugnance for the birthmark that makes Georgiana blanch, thus causing the mark to emerge as a sharply-defined blemish against the whiteness of her cheek. Clearly, the birthmark takes on its character from the eye of the beholder. And just as clearly Georgiana's attitude toward her birthmark varies in response to different observers and definers. Her self-image derives from internalizing the attitudes toward her of the man or men around her. Since what surrounds Georgiana is an obsessional attraction expressed as a total revulsion, the result is not surprising: continual self-consciousness that leads to a pervasive sense of shame and a self-hatred that terminates in an utter readiness to be killed. "The Birthmark" demonstrates the consequences to women of being trapped in the laboratory of man's mind, the object of unrelenting scrutiny, examination, and experimentation.

In addition, "The Birthmark" reveals an implicit understanding of the consequences for women of a linguistic system in which the word "man" refers to both male people and all people. Because of the conventions of this system, Aylmer is able to equate his peculiarly male needs with the needs of all human beings, men and women. And since Aylmer can present his compulsion to idealize and perfect Georgiana as a human aspiration, Georgiana is forced to identify with it . Yet to identify with his aspiration is in fact to identify with his hatred of her and his need to eliminate her. Georgiana's situation is a fictional version of the experience that women undergo when they read a story like "Rip Van Winkle." Under the influence of Aylmer's mind, in the laboratory where she is subjected to his subliminal messages, Georgiana is co-opted into a view of herself as flawed and comes to hate herself as an impediment to Aylmer's aspiration; eventually she wishes to be dead rather than to remain alive as an irritant to him and as a reminder of his failure. And as she identifies with him in her attitude toward herself, so she comes to worship him for his hatred of her and for his refusal to tolerate her existence. The process of projection is neatly reversed: he locates in her everything he cannot accept in himself, and she attributes to him all that is good and then worships in him the image of her own humanity.

Through the system of sexual politics that is Aylmer's compensation for growing up, Hawthorne shows how men gain power over women, the power to create and kill, to "mar," "mend," and "make," without ever having to relinquish their image as "nice guys." Under such a system there need be very few power struggles, because women are programmed to deny the validity of their own perceptions and responses and to accept male illusions as truth. Georgiana does faint when she first enters Aylmer's laboratory and sees it for one second with her own eyes; she is also aware that Aylmer is filling her chamber with appearances, not realities; and she is finally aware that his scientific record is in his own terms one of continual failure. Yet so perfect is the program that she comes to respect him even more for these failures and to aspire to be yet another of them.

Hawthorne's unrelenting emphasis on "seems" and his complex use of the metaphors and structures of disguise imply that women are being deceived and destroyed by man's system. And perhaps the most vicious part of this system is its definition of what constitutes nobility in women: "Drink, then, thou lofty creature," exclaims Aylmer with "fervid admiration" as he hands Georgiana the cup that will kill her. Loftiness in women is directly equivalent to the willingness with which they die at the hands of their husbands, and since such loftiness is the only thing about Georgiana which does elicit admiration from Aylmer, it is no wonder she is willing. Georgiana plays well the one role allowed her, yet one might be justified in suggesting that Hawthorne grants her at the end a slight touch of the satisfaction of revenge: "'My poor Aylmer,' she repeated, with a more than human tenderness, you have aimed loftily; you have done nobly. Do not repent that with so high and pure a feeling, you have rejected the best the earth could offer.'" Since dying is the only option, best to make the most of it.

A Rose for
"A Rose for Emily"

In "A Rose for Emily" the grotesque reality implicit in Aylmer's idealization of Georgiana becomes explicit. Justifying Faulkner's use of the grotesque has been a major concern of critics who have written on the story. If, however, one approaches "A Rose for Emily" from a feminist perspective, one notices that the grotesque aspects of the story are a result of its violation of the expectations generated by the conventions of sexual politics. The ending shocks us not simply by its hint of necrophilia; more shocking is the fact that it is a woman who provides the hint. It is one thing for Poe to spend his nights in the tomb of Annabel Lee and another thing for Miss Emily Grierson to deposit a strand of iron-gray hair on the pillow beside the rotted corpse of Homer Barron. Further, we do not expect to discover that a woman has murdered a man. The conventions of sexual politics have familiarized us with the image of Georgiana nobly accepting death at her husband's hand. To reverse this "natural" pattern inevitably produces the grotesque.

Faulkner, however, is not interested in invoking the kind of grotesque which is the consequence of reversing the clichés of sexism for the sake of a cheap thrill; that is left to writers like Mickey Spillane. (Indeed, Spillane's ready willingness to capitalize on the shock value provided by the image of woman as killer in *I, the Jury* suggests, by contrast, how little such a sexist gambit is Faulkner's intent.) Rather, Faulkner invokes the grotesque in order to illuminate and define the true nature of the conventions on which it depends. "A Rose for Emily" is a story not of a conflict between the South and the North or between the

old order and the new; it is a story of the patriarchy North
and South, new and old, and of the sexual conflict within
it. As Faulkner himself has implied,[10] it is a story of a
woman victimized and betrayed by the system of sexual
politics, who nevertheless has discovered, within the structures that victimize her, sources of power for herself. If
"The Birthmark" is the story of how to murder your wife
and get away with it, "A Rose for Emily" is the story of how
to murder your gentleman caller and get away with it.
Faulkner's story is an analysis of how men's attitudes
toward women turn back upon themselves; it is a demonstration of the thesis that it is impossible to oppress without
in turn being oppressed, it is impossible to kill without
creating the conditions for your own murder. "A Rose for
Emily" is the story of a *lady* and of her revenge for that
grotesque identity.

"When Miss Emily Grierson died, our whole town went
to her funeral." The public and communal nature of Emily's funeral, a festival that brings the town together, clarifying its social relationships and revitalizing its sense of the
past, indicates her central role in Jefferson. Alive, Emily is
town property and the subject of shared speculation; dead,
she is town history and the subject of legend. It is her value
as a symbol, however obscure and however ambivalent, of
something that is of central significance to the identity of
Jefferson and to the meaning of its history that compels
the narrator to assume a communal voice to tell her story.
For Emily, like Georgiana, is a man-made object, a cultural
artifact, and what she is reflects and defines the culture
that has produced her.

The history the narrator relates to us reveals Jefferson's
continuous emotional involvement with Emily. Indeed,
though she shuts herself up in a house which she rarely
leaves and which no one enters, her furious isolation is in
direct proportion to the town's obsession with her. Like
Georgiana, she is the object of incessant attention; her

every act is immediately consumed by the town for gossip
and seized on to justify their interference in her affairs.
Her private life becomes a public document that the town
folk feel free to interpret at will, and they are alternately
curious, jealous, spiteful, pitying, partisan, proud, disap-
proving, admiring, and vindicated. Her funeral is not
simply a communal ceremony; it is also the climax of their
invasion of her private life and the logical extension of
their voyeuristic attitude toward her. Despite the narrator's demurral, getting inside Emily's house is the all-
consuming desire of the town's population, both male and
female; while the men may wait a little longer, their motive
is still prurient curiosity: "Already we knew that there was
one room in that region above stairs which no one had
seen in forty years, and which would have to be forced.
They waited until Miss Emily was decently in the ground
before they opened it."

In a context in which the overtones of violation and
invasion are so palpable, the word "decently" has that
ironic ring which gives the game away. When the men
finally do break down the door, they find that Emily has
satisfied their prurience with a vengeance and in doing so
has created for them a mirror image of themselves. The
true nature of Emily's relation to Jefferson is contained in
the analogies between what those who break open that
room see in it and what has brought them there to see it.
The perverse, violent, and grotesque aspects of the sight of
Homer Barron's rotted corpse in a room decked out for a
bridal and now faded and covered in dust reflects back to
them the perverseness of their own prurient interest in
Emily, the violence implicit in their continued invasions of
her life, and the grotesqueness of the symbolic artifact they
have made of her—their monument, their idol, their lady.
Thus, the figure that Jefferson places at the center of its
legendary history does indeed contain the clue to the
meaning of that history—a history which began long

before Emily's funeral and long before Homer Barron's disappearance or appearance and long before Colonel Sartoris' fathering of edicts and remittances. It is recorded in that emblem which lies at the heart of the town's memory and at the heart of patriarchal culture: "We had long thought of them as a tableau, Miss Emily a slender figure in white in the background, her father a spraddled silhouette in the foreground, his back to her and clutching a horsewhip, the two of them framed by the back-flung front door."

The importance of Emily's father in shaping the quality of her life is insistent throughout the story. Even in her death the force of his presence is felt; above her dead body sits "the crayon face of her father musing profoundly," symbolic of the degree to which he has dominated and shadowed her life, "as if that quality of her father which had thwarted her woman's life so many times had been too virulent and too furious to die." The violence of this consuming relationship is made explicit in the imagery of the tableau. Although the violence is apparently directed outward—the upraised horsewhip against the would-be suitor—the real object of it is the woman–daughter, forced into the background and dominated by the phallic figure of the spraddled father whose back is turned on her and who prevents her from getting out at the same time that he prevents them from getting in. Like Georgiana's spatial confinement in "The Birthmark," Emily's is a metaphor for her psychic confinement: her identity is determined by the constructs of her father's mind, and she can no more escape from his creation of her as "a slender figure in white" than she can escape his house.

What is true for Emily in relation to her father is equally true for her in relation to Jefferson: her status as a lady is a cage from which she cannot escape. To them she is always *Miss* Emily; she is never referred to and never thought of as otherwise. In omitting her title from his, Faulkner emphasizes the point that the real violence done to Emily is in making her a "Miss"; the omission is one of his roses for her. Because she is *Miss* Emily *Grierson,* Emily's father dresses her in white, places her in the background, and drives away her suitors. Because she is Miss Emily Grierson, the town invests her with that communal significance which makes her the object of their obsession and the subject of their incessant scrutiny. And because she is a lady, the town is able to impose a particular code of behavior on her ("But there were still others, older people, who said that even grief could not cause a real lady to forget *noblesse oblige*") and to see in her failure to live up to that code an excuse for interfering in her life. As a lady, Emily is venerated, but veneration results in the more telling emotions of envy and spite: "It was another link between the gross, teeming world and the high and mighty Griersons"; "People . . . believed that the Griersons held themselves a little too high for what they really were." The violence implicit in the desire to see the monument fall and reveal itself for clay suggests the violence inherent in the original impulse to venerate.

The violence behind veneration is emphasized through another telling emblem in the story. Emily's position as an hereditary obligation upon the town dates from "that day in 1894 when Colonel Sartoris, the mayor—he who fathered the edict that no Negro woman should appear on the streets without an apron on—remitted her taxes, the dispensation dating from the death of her father on into perpetuity." The conjunction of these two actions in the same syntactic unit is crucial, for it insists on their essential similarity. It indicates that the impulse to exempt is analogous to the desire to restrict, and that what appears to be a kindness or an act of veneration is in fact an insult. Sartoris' remission of Emily's taxes is a public declaration of the fact that a lady is not considered to be, and hence not allowed or enabled to be, economically independent (consider, in this connection, Emily's lessons in china painting; they are a latter-day version of Sartoris' "charity" and a brilliant image of Emily's economic uselessness). His act is a public statement of the fact that a lady, if she is to survive, must have either husband or father, and that, because Emily has neither, the town must assume responsibility for her. The remission of taxes that defines Emily's status dates from the death of her father, and she is handed over from one patron to the next, the town instead of husband taking on the role of father. Indeed, the use of the word "fathered" in describing Sartoris' behavior as mayor underlines the fact that his chivalric attitude toward Emily is simply a subtler and more dishonest version of her father's horsewhip.

The narrator is the last of the patriarchs who take upon themselves the burden of defining Emily's life, and his violence toward her is the most subtle of all. His tone of incantatory reminiscence and nostalgic veneration seems free of the taint of horsewhip and edict. Yet a thoroughgoing contempt for the "ladies" who spy and pry and gossip out of their petty jealousy and curiosity is one of the clearest strands in the narrator's consciousness. Emily is exempted from the general indictment because she is a *real* lady—that is, eccentric, slightly crazy, obsolete, a "stubborn and coquettish decay," absurd but indulged; "dear, inescapable, impervious, tranquil, and perverse"; indeed, anything and everything but human.

Not only does "A Rose for Emily" expose the violence done to a woman by making her a lady; it also explores the particular form of power the victim gains from this position and can use on those who enact this violence. "A Rose for Emily" is concerned with the consequences of violence for both the violated and the violators. One of the most striking aspects of the story is the disparity between Miss Emily Grierson and the Emily to whom Faulkner gives his rose in ironic imitation of the chivalric behavior the story exposes. The form of Faulkner's title establishes a camaraderie between author and protagonist and signals that a distinction must be made between the story Faulkner is telling and the story the narrator is telling. This distinction is of major importance because it suggests, of course, that the narrator, looking through a patriarchal lens, does not see Emily at all but rather a figment of his own imagination created in conjunction with the cumulative imagination of the town. Like Ellison's invisible man, nobody sees *Emily*. And because nobody sees *her*, she can literally get away with murder. Emily is characterized by her ability to understand and utilize the power that accrues to her from the fact that men do not see her but rather their concept of her: "'I have no taxes in Jefferson. Colonel Sartoris explained it to me. . . . Tobe! . . . Show these gentlemen out.'" Relying on the conventional assumptions about ladies who are expected to be neither reasonable nor in touch with reality, Emily presents an impregnable front that vanquishes the men "horse and foot, just as she had vanquished their fathers thirty years before." In spite of their "modern" ideas, this new generation, when faced with Miss Emily, are as much bound by the code of gentlemanly behavior as their fathers were ("They rose when she entered"). This code gives Emily a power that renders the gentlemen unable to function in a situation in which a lady neither sits down herself nor asks them to. They are brought to a "stumbling halt" and can do nothing when confronted with her refusal to engage in rational discourse. Their only recourse in the face of such eccentricity is to engage in behavior unbecoming to gentlemen, and Emily can count on their continuing to see themselves as gentlemen and her as a lady and on their returning a verdict of helpless noninterference.

It is in relation to Emily's disposal of Homer Barron, however, that Faulkner demonstrates most clearly the power of conventional assumptions about the nature of

ladies to blind the town to what is going on and to allow
Emily to murder with impunity. When Emily buys the
poison, it never occurs to anyone that she intends to use it
on Homer, so strong is the presumption that ladies when
jilted commit suicide, not murder. And when her house
begins to smell, the women blame it on the eccentricity of
having a man servant rather than a woman, "as if a man—
any man—could keep a kitchen properly." And then they
hint that her eccentricity may have shaded over into madness, "remembering how old lady Wyatt, her great aunt,
had gone completely crazy at last." The presumption of
madness, that preeminently female response to bereave-
ment, can be used to explain away much in the behavior of
ladies whose activities seem a bit odd.

But even more pointed is what happens when the men
try not to explain but to do something about the smell:
" 'Dammit, sir,' Judge Stevens said, 'will you accuse a lady
to her face of smelling bad?'" But if a lady cannot be told
that she smells, then the cause of the smell cannot be discovered and so her crime is "perfect." Clearly, the assumptions behind the Judge's outraged retort go beyond the
myth that ladies are out of touch with reality. His outburst
insists that it is the responsibility of gentlemen to make
them so. Ladies must not be confronted with facts; they
must be shielded from all that is unpleasant. Thus Colonel
Sartoris remits Emily's taxes with a palpably absurd story,
designed to protect her from an awareness of her poverty
and her dependence on charity, and to protect him from
having to confront her with it. And thus Judge Stevens will
not confront Emily with the fact that her house stinks,
though she is living in it and can hardly be unaware of the
odor. Committed as they are to the myth that ladies and
bad smells cannot coexist, these gentlemen insulate themselves from reality. And by defining a lady as a subhuman
and hence sublegal entity, they have created a situation
their laws can't touch. They have made it possible for

Emily to be extra-legal: "'Why, of course,' the druggist
said, 'If that's what you want. But the law requires you to
tell what you are going to use it for.' Miss Emily just stared
at him, her head tilted back in order to look him eye for
eye, until he looked away and went and got the arsenic and
wrapped it up." And, finally, they have created a situation
in which they become the criminals: "So the next night,
after midnight, four men crossed Miss Emily's lawn and
slunk about the house like burglars." Above them, "her
upright torso motionless as that of an idol," sits Emily,
observing them act out their charade of chivalry. As they
leave, she confronts them with the reality they are trying to
protect her from: she turns on the light so that they may
see her watching them. One can only wonder at the fact,
and regret, that she didn't call the sheriff and have them
arrested for trespassing.

Not only is "A Rose for Emily" a supreme analysis of
what men do to women by making them ladies; it is also an
exposure of how this act in turn defines and recoils upon
men. This is the significance of the dynamic that Faulkner
establishes between Emily and Jefferson. And it is equally
the point of the dynamic implied between the tableau of
Emily and her father and the tableau which greets the men
who break down the door of that room in the region above
the stairs. When the would-be "suitors" finally get into her
father's house, they discover the consequences of his oppression of her, for the violence contained in the rotted
corpse of Homer Barron is the mirror image of the violence represented in the tableau, the back-flung front door
flung back with a vengeance. Having been consumed by
her father, Emily in turn feeds off Homer Barron, becoming, after his death, suspiciously fat. Or, to put it another
way, it is as if, after her father's death, she has reversed his
act of incorporating her by incorporating and becoming
him, metamorphosed from the slender figure in white to
the obese figure in black whose hair is "a vigorous iron-

gray, like the hair of an active man." She has taken into herself the violence in him which thwarted her and has reenacted it upon Homer Barron.

That final encounter, however, is not simply an image of the reciprocity of violence. Its power of definition also derives from its grotesqueness, which makes finally explicit the grotesqueness that has been latent in the description of Emily throughout the story: "Her skeleton was small and spare; perhaps that was why what would have been merely plumpness in another was obesity in her. She looked bloated, like a body long submerged in motionless water, and of that pallid hue. Her eyes, lost in the fatty ridges of her face, looked like two small pieces of coal pressed into a lump of dough." The impact of this description depends on the contrast it establishes between Emily's reality as a fat, bloated figure in black and the conventional image of a lady—expectations that are fostered in the town by its emblematic memory of Emily as a slender figure in white and in us by the narrator's tone of romantic invocation and by the passage itself. Were she not expected to look so different, were her skeleton not small and spare, Emily would not be so grotesque. Thus, the focus is on the grotesqueness that results when stereotypes are imposed upon reality. And the implication of this focus is that the real grotesque is the stereotype itself. If Emily is both lady and grotesque, then the syllogism must be completed thus: the idea of a lady is grotesque. So Emily is metaphor and mirror for the town of Jefferson; and when, at the end, the town folk finally discover who and what she is, they have in fact encountered who and what they are.

Despite similarities of focus and vision, "A Rose for Emily" is more implicitly feminist than "The Birthmark." For one thing, Faulkner does not have Hawthorne's compulsive ambivalence; one is not invited to misread "A Rose for Emily" as one is invited to misread "The Birthmark."

Thus, the interpretation of "The Birthmark" that sees it as a story of misguided idealism, despite its massive oversights, nevertheless *works;* while the efforts to read "A Rose for Emily" as a parable of the relations between North and South, or as a conflict between an old order and a new, or as a story about the human relation to Time, don't work because the attempt to make Emily representative of such concepts stumbles over the fact that woman's condition is not the "human" condition.[11] To understand Emily's experience requires a primary awareness of the fact that she is a woman.

But, more important, Faulkner provides us with an image of retaliation. Unlike Georgiana, Emily does not simply acquiesce; she prefers to murder rather than to die. In this respect she is a welcome change from the image of woman as willing victim that fills the pages of our literature, and whose other face is the ineffective fulminations of Dame Van Winkle. Nevertheless, Emily's action is still reaction. "A Rose for Emily" exposes the poverty of a situation in which turnabout is the only possibility and in which one's acts are neither self-generated nor self-determined but are simply a response to and a reflection of forces outside oneself. Though Emily may be proud, strong, and indomitable, her murder of Homer Barron is finally an indication of the severely limited nature of the power women can wrest from the system that oppresses them. Aylmer's murder of Georgiana is an indication of men's absolute power over women; it is an act performed in the complete security of his ability to legitimize it as a noble and human pursuit. Emily's act has no such context. It is possible only because it can be kept secret; and it can be kept secret only at the cost of exploiting her image as a lady. Furthermore, Aylmer murders Georgiana in order to get rid of her; Emily murders Homer Barron in order to have him.

Patriarchal culture is based to a considerable extent on

the argument that men and women are made for each other and on the conviction that "masculinity" and "femininity" are the natural reflection of that divinely ordained complement. Yet, if one reads "The Birthmark" and "A Rose for Emily" as analyses of the consequences of a massive differentiation of everything according to sex, one sees that in reality a sexist culture is one in which men and women are not simply incompatible but murderously so. Aylmer murders Georgianna because he must at any cost get rid of woman; Emily murders Homer Barron because she must at any cost get a man. The two stories define the disparity between cultural myth and cultural reality, and they suggest that in this disparity is the ultimate grotesque.

A FAREWELL TO ARMS
Hemingway's
"Resentful Cryptogram"

I

Once upon a time there was a writer who told the truth. He wrote a story called "Indian Camp" and in that story a little boy watches his doctor–father perform a contemptuous and grotesque Caesarean section on an Indian woman while her husband in the bunk above slits his throat. Like "I Want to Know Why," "Indian Camp" is a story of initiation, and in it Nick Adams is given a lesson in the meaning of growing up male in America: "'That's one for the medical journal, George,' he said. 'Doing a Caesarean with a jack-knife and sewing it up with nine-foot, tapered gut leaders.'" The lesson, reflected in the double mirror of the two fathers, is one of guilt—guilt for the attitudes men have toward women and guilt for the consequences to women of male sexuality. *A Farewell to Arms* has many of the same elements as "Indian Camp" but they are significantly rearranged. There is still the painful and protracted labor followed by the Caesarean birth of a son, but the emotions which surround this event have been displaced from the self onto the other. The hostility toward the father in "Indian Camp" is now directed against Catherine, the woman, and it is her sexuality, her strangling womb, which is the enemy. And the guilt which in "Indian Camp" is so clearly located in the male self of the Indian father has been deflected onto Catherine, who takes upon herself the burden of Frederic's sins and dies for him.

In comparison to "Indian Camp," *A Farewell to Arms* is a lie. Yet the lie is a familiar one to anyone who knows the tradition and the mentality that inform "Rip Van Winkle," "I Want to Know Why," and "The Birthmark." "Indian Camp" ends with its protagonist in a state of limbo; he has rejected his father and retreated from reality. *A Farewell to Arms* portrays that protagonist in the escape route provided by nominal adulthood, a route that involves the strategy of projection, the mechanism of the scapegoat, and the creation of a mythology which allows for the evasion of one's true motives and true aim. And Frederic Henry's true aim, as it finally is Aylmer's, is to resolve the dilemma documented in "I Want to Know Why" and "Indian Camp" by evading the fact of growing up and by eliminating the agent that threatens to force adulthood upon one. Like Rip Van Winkle, Frederic Henry sleeps a lot, and the dream he dreams is the archetypal American one of remaining forever a boy in an asexual world without women.

Aylmer's mythology is science; Frederic Henry's is romantic love. Both are processes of idealization which serve to disguise hostility. Since *A Farewell to Arms* is written in the tradition of romantic love, it will be worthwhile to examine briefly some of the elements of this tradition, for love stories are perhaps the ultimate form of disguise and deception. When I first read Erich Segal's *Love Story*, I was struck by its similarity to *A Farewell to Arms*. Both novels are characterized by a disparity between what is overtly stated and what is covertly expressed. Both ask the reader to believe in the perfection of a love whose substance seems woefully inadequate and whose signature is death. "What can you say about a twenty-five-year-old girl who died?" asks Oliver Barrett IV on the opening page of *Love Story.* The answer is, as the question implies, not very much, because the investment of this love story, like so many others, is not in the life of the beloved but in her death and in the emotional rewards the hero gets from that death—Oliver Barrett weeping in the arms of his long-estranged but now-reconciled father. What one doesn't say is precisely that which alone would be worth saying: that you loved her because she died or, conversely, that because you loved her she died. For surely one of the central questions that such love stories raise is why their emotional charge so often depends on the death of the woman and so rarely on the death of the man. Why the death of a beautiful woman, as Poe suggested, should be such an unfailing source of "universal" melancholy is a question well worth pondering. Certainly one of its implications is that the tears are a luxury enjoyed by the survivor, who is male or male-identified, and that at some level the experience is factitious and dishonest.

If we examine Hemingway's novel closely, we will discover that the emotions which in fact direct it are quite opposite from those which are claimed as central. One cannot miss the disparity between the novel's overt fabric of idealized romance and its underlying vision of the radical limitations of love, between its surface idyll and its subsurface critique. And one is equally struck by its heavy use of the metaphor and motif of disguise. When Sheridan Baker describes *A Farewell to Arms* as a "resentful cryptogram," he is essentially extending this metaphor to the form of the novel itself.[1] That deviousness and indirection are often the companions of hostility is no new observation, and that idealization often disguises and masks hatred is clear from our reading of "The Birthmark." If we explore the attitude toward women in *A Farewell to Arms,* we will discover that while the novel's surface investment is in idealization, behind that idealization is a hostility whose full measure can be taken from the fact that Catherine dies and dies because she is a woman.

The disparity between the claimed and the real is also apparent from the novel's subject matter, the joining of the twin themes of love and war. We are told that love and war are "strange but time-honored bed-companions,"[2] and that "despite the frequency with which they appear in the same books, the themes of love and war are really an unlikely pair, if not indeed—to judge from the frequency with which writers fail to wed them—quite incompatible."[3] Nevertheless, many of the interpreters of *A Farewell to Arms* have sought to provide a framework within which these apparently irreconcilable subjects do, in fact, make sense. We may, therefore, be justified if we pause for a moment to raise a question, and an eyebrow, at the remarks quoted above of Robert W. Lewis, Jr., and Philip Young. Is it entirely accidental that both of them invoke a sexual metaphor to describe what they think cannot be made to go together? If metaphor is indeed itself a cryptogram, may we not be justified in decoding thus: love and war appear together so frequently because romantic love is a form of war? Such a reading would seem to be invited by the title of the novel, whose pun suggests, despite its sentimental intention, that the arms of war and the arms of love are equivalent. Thus, the world of the Italian front is not contrast but complement to Frederic and Catherine's love and is the best place to begin our exploration of the meaning of that emotion.

War simplifies men's relation to women.[4] It erases the distinctions among women that normally keep male hostility under some restraint and it legitimizes aggression against all women. The fear in the eyes of the virgins whom Frederic picks up during the retreat registers their

acute awareness of the position of women in war. The
virgins know that there is only one category for them in
this world and that is the category of sexual object: whores
if they are picked up by their own side, victims of rape if
they are captured by the enemy, though even this marginal distinction is often violated. The initial complication
Catherine Barkley introduces is being a nurse in a world
where all women are whores. The Italians don't want
nurses at the front and don't know what to do with them.
Rinaldi makes a brief attempt to accommodate Catherine
through the fantasy of marriage, after which he resolves
his dilemma in the fashion of the other Italians by turning
nurses into a sexual category and viewing them solely in
sexual terms: "'What a lovely girl. . . . Does she understand
that? She will make you a fine boy. A fine blonde like she is.
. . . What a lovely girl'" (A Farewell to Arms, [1929; rpt.
N.Y.: Scribner, 1957], p. 99). One asks of doctors if they
are good at surgery, if they will make you a fine leg; one
asks of nurses if they are sexually adequate, if they will
make you a fine boy. Rinaldi asks one question about
Catherine when Frederic returns to the front after his
hospitalization in Milan: "'I mean is she good to you prac-
tically speaking'" (p. 169), that is, does she go down on
you? Is she a good whore?
  Rinaldi's refusal to see women in other than sexual
terms is quite clear from his outburst to Frederic before
the latter leaves for Milan:

Your lovely cool goddess. English goddess. My God what
would a man do with a woman like that except worship her?
What else is an Englishwoman good for? . . . I tell you something about your good women. Your goddesses. There is
only one difference between taking a girl who has always
been good and a woman. With a girl it is painful. . . . And
you never know if the girl will really like it.

                                              (p. 66)

The implications are that if a woman is good only for worship, then she really isn't any good at all, because women exist only for one thing and the real definition of a good woman is she who knows what she exists for and does it and lets you know that she likes it. Any woman who wishes to think of herself in other than sexual terms is denying her humanness and trying to be superhuman, a goddess, for humanness in women is synonymous with being sexual.

The contempt and hostility Rinaldi feels for women who dare to be more than sexual are directed also against women who are only sexual. The emotions of his reductive paradigm also define scenes like the one in which the soldiers watch their whores being loaded into a truck for the retreat: "I'd like to be there when some of those tough babies climb in and try and hop them. . . . I'd like to have a crack at them for nothing. They charge too much at that house anyway. The government gyps us" (p. 189). Herded like animals, the whores are seen by the men as so many pieces of meat whose price on the market is too damn high for what they get. Because, after all, what *do* they get? "Over in half an hour or fifteen minutes. Sometimes less. Sometimes a good deal less" (pp. 170-71). And the result? Syphilis and gonorrhea. This attitude toward women has its obvious correlative in an attitude toward sexuality. Coarse, gross, the favorite subject matter for jokes whose hostility is hardly worth disguising, sex is seen as the antithesis of sensitivity, tenderness, idealism, and ultimately of knowledge. When the men in Frederic Henry's "mess" bait their priest with endless sexual jokes, they are expressing their sense of his difference and their uneasiness in the face of it. For, by virtue of his asexuality, the priest has access to a certain knowledge and stature that the men who remain sexual do not have and secretly admire. "He had always known what I did not know and what, when I learned it, I was always able to forget" (p. 14). The priest, who comes from the cold, white , pure mountainous world of the Abruzzi, where women are safely distanced and men relate to each other,[5] knows something that Frederic Henry, who is down there on the plain among the whores, who "had gone to no such place but to the smoke of cafés and nights when the room whirled and you needed to look at the wall to make it stop" (p. 13), does not know and who, when he learns it, cannot hold on to: that sex is a dangerous and wasteful commodity and the best world is one of men without women. The priest alone is able to carry out the full implications of his culture's attitude toward sex.

II

On first consideration, Frederic Henry seems to be quite different from his companions at the front. His position as an American fighting in an Italian war would seem to be a metaphor for his larger role of outsider in this culture, for he is sensitive and tender, capable of a sustained personal relationship with a woman and of an idealization of love that appears to be the secular analogue of the priest's asexual spirituality. While he does not openly identify with the cleric, neither does he join his mess-mates in their priest-baiting. Catherine is for him a "sacred subject," and he resists Rinaldi's attempt to sexualize everything and to reduce his feeling for Catherine to the genitals. At one point, when Catherine is teasing Frederic, she refers to him as "Othello with his occupation gone" (p. 257). The allusion is striking because it suggests how different Frederic is from the culture in which he finds himself. He is neither Othello as soldier nor Othello as lover; it is impossible to imagine him strangling Catherine in a fit of jealous rage. But when one considers the events of *A Farewell to Arms*, one is tempted to speculate that the difference between Frederic and Othello is essentially superficial and rests only in the degree to which each is able to face his immense egocentrism and the extent to which that egocentrism is responsible for the death of his "beloved." If the violence of the novel's ending is striking, so too is its abstract nature, its reliance on a biological trap which is the agent of an impersonal "they" who break the brave and beautiful. Yet surely this abstraction masks both Frederic's fear of Catherine and his hostility toward her. The image of strangulation, suggested by the comparison with Othello, persists, leaving in us the nagging suspicion that Frederic Henry sees himself in the dead fetus which emerges from Catherine's womb and that her death, however much it may be shaped as biological accident, is in fact the fulfillment of his own unconscious wish, his need to kill her lest she kill him.[6]

Frederic Henry's hostility to women is in some ways quite open, especially during his encounters with women in positions of authority. Like Rinaldi, who resents women who try to be goddesses, Frederic resents women who do not present themselves primarily as love objects. While Frederic's enmity finds overt expression only rarely—e.g., at the end of the novel when he shoves the two nurses out of the room in order to make his peace with the dead Catherine—it is implicit in his view of these women as smug, self-righteous, critical, antisexual, and sadistic; and he conveys it through his reactions to them. Consider, for instance, his exchange with the head nurse at the hospital where Catherine works when first at the front. In response to his request for Catherine, he is informed that she is on duty, and, the nurse adds, "there's a war on, you know" (p. 22). By implication Frederic is defined as an egocentric, insensitive noncombatant who expects to get his pleasure while other men are dying. This woman speaks from a presumed moral superiority, which she uses to humiliate Frederic.

The hostility between Frederic and women in authority comes out more fully in his relation to Miss Van Campen, the head of the hospital in Milan to which he is taken after his injury. Their dislike for each other is immediate and instinctual, as if each realizes in the other a natural enemy. When she describes Frederic as "domineering and rude," she defines the nature of their relationship as a power struggle. Not the least bit impressed by her authority or her rules, Frederic thoroughly discredits the one and pays no attention to the other: "She was small and neatly suspicious and too good for her position. She asked many questions and seemed to think it was somewhat disgraceful that I was with the Italians" (p. 86). Like the earlier nurse, Van Campen sees herself as morally superior to Frederic and is critical of him, seeing in him a selfish egotist, as insensitive to the concerns of others as he is to the larger issue of the war. But Frederic disarms her criticism by implying that the basis of her hostility toward him is his sexual relation with Catherine. He places her in the category, so comfortable to the male ego, of the frustrated old maid who, because she has never had sex, is jealous of those who do and persecutes them. He insinuates that her hostility results from rejection while his is the result of contempt.

In the final phase of their struggle, Frederic employs the method by which men have classically sought to deny women any possibility of power, authority, or credibility. He denies her ability to be a judge of male experience by reminding her that she is not a man and by calling into question her sexuality and her status as a woman. All Frederic feels he need do to rout her utterly is to imply that she is not a full woman, that she has had no sexual experience, and that she knows nothing of the pain of the scrotum or the agonies of the womb. So insecure as a person because she has failed to be a woman, she can in Frederic's eyes be vanquished by the merest mention of the sacred genitalia. The perfect chauvinist, Frederic uses his penis as the ultimate weapon and the ultimate court of appeal.

Although Frederic Henry does not like women who aspire to positions of authority, neither does he like women who are incompetent. Doing night duty in a just-opened and empty hospital, Mrs. Walker is awakened from her sleep to deal with an unexpected patient and proves to be unable to handle the situation: "I don't know," "I couldn't put you in just any room," "I can't put on sheets," "I can't read Italian," "I can't do anything without the doctor's orders" (pp. 82, 83). Frederic is contemptuous of her incompetence and deals with it by ignoring her and turning to the men involved, who, despite their being mere porters, are able to get him to a bed. Mrs. Walker is one of a number of weepy women in the novel who appear to have no way of meeting difficulty other than by crying. The attitude toward them is one in which contempt is mingled with patronizing pity. Poor Mrs. Walker, poor Fergy, poor whores, poor virgins. Here, of course, is a classic instance of the double bind: women are pathetic in their inability to handle difficulty, but if they assume positions of authority and, even worse, use the authority conferred by those positions, they become unbearably self-righteous and superior. Damned if you do and damned if you don't. But ultimately less damned if you don't, because at least Walker is a Mrs.—no shadow here of not being a real woman—while it is Van Campen who bears the stigma of Miss. Frederic Henry is finally more comfortable with women who do not threaten his ego by pretending to authority over him. This is part of his attraction to whores: "'Does she [the whore] say she loves him?' . . . 'Yes. If *he* wants her to.' 'Does he say he loves her?' . . . 'He does if *he* wants to'" (p. 105, italics mine).

III

The context within which the great love of Frederic Henry and Catherine Barkley occurs is one of multiple hostilities. If we examine the origins of this emotion, we will begin to expose the degree to which it is in fact complement rather than contrast to this context. Despite the mythology around the phenomenon of falling in love that defines it as an accident over which one has no control, anyone who examines her or his history carefully might be more inclined to say that there is nothing less arbitrary in all one's experience than falling in love. While Frederic Henry views his experience with Catherine as something that happens to him, describing it in terms of the trap metaphor elaborated in the novel, it seems clear that he falls in love when he needs to and with whom. Certainly it is not fortuitous that it happens after Frederic is wounded, when his disillusionment with the arms of war is growing daily and when he is particularly in need of the alternate experience that will eventually justify his flight from the world of war. Nor is it fortuitous that it occurs when he is most in need of the loving service Nurse Barkley is so willing to provide. Frederic has, after all, had several weeks of lying flat on his back with a smashed leg and little else to think about except the absurdity of his position in relation to the war, his isolation, and the essential fragility of life. Such thoughts might incline one to accept affection and service even if they require the word "love" to get them. And Frederic, trapped as he is in a cast, in a bed, in a hospital, in a stupid war, seems only too happy to avail himself of Catherine's service: "Catherine Barkley was greatly liked by the nurses because she would do night duty indefinitely" (p. 108). Frederic greatly likes her for this, too, since it means she is available for his needs not only during the day but all night as well. While Frederic sleeps, however, Catherine goes right on working. He is conveniently unaware of her exhaustion in the face of the double duty induced by his continual invitations to "play," until Catherine's friend, Ferguson, points it out to him and insists that he get her to take a rest.

That egotism is the root of Frederic's feeling for Catherine is clear, too, in those few scenes in which Catherine makes demands on Frederic. During their second meeting, Frederic tries to kiss Catherine. Because she feels that he is insincere, that his gesture is simply part of the routine soldiers go through when they get a nurse on her evening off, she says no; and when that has no effect, she slaps him. Frederic responds to her initial refusal by ignoring it. When she slaps him, he gets angry and uses his anger in combination with her guilt to get what he wanted in the first place. Jackson J. Benson describes the situation accurately:

> In his early encounters with the British nurse Catherine Barkley, Henry is the casual, uniformed boy on the make, but down deep inside he is really a decent sort. In other words, what makes Henry so sinister is his All-American-Boy lack of guile. He demonstrates an attitude and pattern of behavior that any Rotarian would privately endorse. He fully intends (he spells it out quite clearly) to take a girl, who is described in terms of a helpless, trembling Henry James bird, and crush her in his hands very casually as part of the game that every young, virile lad must play. It is a backhanded tribute to Hemingway's irony here that most readers don't seem to even blanch at the prospect.[7]

But if irony is so unrecognizable, one is justified in questioning whether or not it is intended. And why should Hemingway in this instance be separated from the cultural norm of "any Rotarian" embodied in Frederic and Catherine's view of the affair. Both of them see Frederic's anger as justifiable, the legitimate response of a male thwarted in his rightful desires by a maiden unduly coy (*vide* Catherine's reference to Marvell's "To His Coy Mistress": "it's about a girl who wouldn't live with a man"), whose posture of trembling helplessness is simply a way of disguising what she really wants or ought to want.

Later in the novel, in the hotel room they have taken to spend a last few hours together before Frederic leaves for the front, Catherine has a sudden attack of depression. The idea of taking a room not for the night but for two or three hours, the quality of the hotel, and the décor of the room all combine to make her feel like a whore. At the moment when Catherine is experiencing this feeling of alienation, Frederic is standing by the windows whose red plush curtains he has just closed, in a gesture that signals their possession of the room as another "home" and encloses the two of them in an inner world that reflects his sense of their closeness. Obviously they are at this moment poles apart in their feelings. Then Frederic catches sight of Catherine in the mirrors which surround the room and discovers that she is unhappy. He is surprised—for how could they be reacting so differently when they two are one and that one is he—and disappointed, for this will upset his plans for their last evening together. "You're not a whore," he says, as if simple assertion were sufficient to cancel the complex sources of her sense of degradation. He then proceeds to register his own feelings of disappointment, anger, and frustration in unmistakable terms: he reopens the curtains and looks out, implying that she has shattered their rapport and broken up their home. Quite literally, Frederic turns his back on Catherine. His meaning is clear. Catherine's unhappiness is something he can respond to only in terms of how it affects him; beyond that, it is her problem and when she gets herself together and is ready to be his "good girl" again, then he will come back. And if she doesn't? "Oh, hell, I thought, do we have to argue now?" (p. 152). Either she does what he wants or he gets angry. Hostility and love seem very close here,

separated only by Catherine's ability to fulfill the demands
of Frederic's ego. Catherine's behavior indicates that she
knows quite well the source of Frederic's love. Supersensi-
tive to his ego, she is forever asking him, "What would you
like me to do now?" And she continually responds to their
situation in terms of his needs: I'll get rid of Ferguson so
that we can go to bed, you must go play with Count Greffi,
don't you want a weekend with the boys, I know I'm not
much fun now that I'm big.

There are, however, even more radical ways in which
Catherine is useful to Frederic and which predicate his
falling in love with her. The essential passivity of Hemingway's protagonist has been amply documented. Among
the "multitudinous ranks of *those to whom things happen*,"
Frederic Henry lacks "executive will," a sense of responsibility and the capacity to make a commitment.[8] In contrast
to Frederic's passivity, Catherine's aggressiveness is striking. How, after all, can a heroine be allowed so much activity and still keep her status as an idealized love object,
especially since Frederic dislikes women with authority?
Catherine's aggressiveness, however, achieves legitimacy
because it is always exercised in the service of Frederic's
passivity. Whenever Catherine acts, she does so in order to
save Frederic from responsibility and commitment. It is
Catherine who creates the involvement between herself
and Frederic: it is she who constructs their initial
encounter in such a way as to place them in a "relationship" almost immediately; it is she who shows up at the
hospital in Milan so that he can fall in love with her. In
addition, Catherine takes full responsibility for the pregnancy and for figuring out where and how she will have
their baby. When she dies, she takes, in conjunction with
certain ill-defined cosmic forces, the responsibility for the
termination of their relationship. It is possible for Frederic
to love Catherine because she provides him with the only
kind of relationship he is capable of accepting: he does not

have to act; he does not have to think about things because
she thinks for him ("You see, darling, if I marry you I'll be
an American and any time we're married under American
law the child is legitimate"); he does not have to assume
responsibility; and he does not have to make a final commitment because both her facile logic and her ultimate
death give him a convenient out.

Frederic's need to avoid responsibility is central to his
character and Catherine is central to that need. He is able
to relate to her precisely because and so long as their relationship has neither past nor future. He is spared complications by Catherine's death in childbirth, that "cloud," as
John Killinger puts it, "spread by the author as a disguise
for pulling off a *deus ex machina* to save his hero from the
existential hell of a complicated life."[9] Through
Catherine's death Frederic Henry avoids having to face
the responsibilities incumbent on a husband and father.
Her death abets his desire to remain uncommitted and
gives him a justification for it.

It is easy to say, however, that in serving Frederic's need
to avoid responsibility and to remain uncommitted
Catherine has failed him. Thus, Robert Lewis can write of
Catherine: "Her death carries the hope with it of the destruction of her destructive love that excludes the world,
that in its denial of self possesses selfishly, that leads
nowhere beyond the bed and the dream of a mystical
transport of ordinary men and women to a divine state of
love through foolish suffering." As Lewis's tone indicates,
Catherine's very adaptability to Frederic's need "to reduce
life to its lowest denominator, to make it simple, to make it
thoughtless, to destroy consciousness and responsibility in
a romantic, orgiastic dream" is in itself a source of his
hostility toward her.[10]

Let us recapitulate. On the simplest level Frederic falls
in love with Catherine because she is useful to him; she
serves his physical needs and adapts herself to his emotional requirements, primary among which is his desire to

avoid responsibility and commitment. But to the degree to which this desire is juvenile, in indulging it she fails him.

But one can give the emotional screw of the novel one final turn. In failing Frederic, Catherine provides the ultimate service. The moral basis of Frederic Henry's resistance to accepting responsibility is his sense that he is a victim of betrayal. Frederic needs to feel betrayed and Catherine serves this need. And he needs to feel betrayed because a sense of betrayal is the structure that supports his ego; it allows him the indulgence of his egotism through the posture of self-pity and provides the justification for his evasion of responsibility. Frederic finds betrayal everywhere. Betrayal is at the heart of his experience in the war; the killings the novel details are those of Italians by Italians, and Frederic makes his break for the river because he is about to be shot by his own army as a traitor. The imagery of betrayal also informs Frederic's concept of Catherine's experience; she is betrayed by her own body, whose physical construction is in direct opposition to its biological function. In internecine strife she destroys herself. Betrayal permeates Frederic's view of nature and is at the root of his vision of the universe as one in which a "we" who are good and brave and beautiful are opposed by a "they" who wish to break us precisely because we are good and brave and beautiful.

Catherine betrays Frederic too. She entangles him in a relationship with her, pretending that there will be no drawbacks, no demands, pressures, or responsibilities, only benefits; then she gets pregnant: "I know I've made trouble now" (p. 138). At one point, early in the novel, when Frederic is going off to see Catherine, he asks Rinaldi to come with him. Rinaldi answers, "No . . . I like the simpler pleasures" (p. 41). To Rinaldi, Catherine is a complication and what she has to offer cannot compensate for the complications that come along with her. Frederic echoes Rinaldi's view of love and women when he says, "God knows I had not wanted to fall in love with her. I had not

wanted to fall in love with anyone" (p. 93). And while at
this moment he claims, in spite of not wanting this complication in his life, to feel "wonderful," at other times he
appears to feel differently. "You always feel trapped
biologically," he says to Catherine, and the announcement
of her pregnancy is followed not only by the rain but by his
waking in the night nauseated and jaundiced. The conjunction is hardly accidental. If in Rinaldi's eyes women
give one syphilis, Catherine, it would seem, makes Frederic sick. Finally, at the end of the novel, after making him
emotionally dependent on her, Catherine abandons Frederic; she dies happily ever after and leaves him alone to
face a cold, wet, hostile world. "There isn't anything, dog,"
Frederic says to a stray nosing a garbage can filled with
coffee grounds, dust, and dead flowers (p. 315). Palpably
self-pitying, Frederic sees himself alone in an empty world
which no longer has nourishment for him. Catherine cuts
off his life as effectively as she strangles her own son inside
her.

But if Catherine is just one more piece of evidence to
validate Frederic's sentimental and egocentric philosophy
that the world exists for the single purpose of breaking
him, then she has once again failed him. *Da capo. Ad
nauseam.* The point is that no matter what Catherine does,
she is bad for Frederic. Her death is the logical consequence of the cumulative hostilities Frederic feels toward
her, and the final expression of the connection between
the themes of love and war.

IV

In *A Farewell to Arms* the connection of sex and death is
made by the second page of the book: "their rifles were wet
and under their capes the two leather cartridge-boxes on

the front of the belts, gray leather boxes heavy with the packs of clips of thin, long 6.5 mm. cartridges, bulged forward under the capes so that the men, passing on the road, marched as though they were six months gone with child." That pregnancy is death and the womb an agent of destruction could hardly be stated more clearly. The real source of betrayal in *A Farewell to Arms* is not simply biology; it is, specifically, female biology. Women, who promise life, are in reality death, and their inner world is finally nightmare. Conversely, the outer world of men, which seems overtly to be given over to death, is finally the reservoir of hope and possibility: "If it is possible, I will return to the Abruzzi."

Very early in *A Farewell to Arms* a contrast is established between outer and inner space. Frederic tries to explain to the priest why he never got back to the Abruzzi, "where the roads were frozen and hard as iron, where it was clear cold and dry and the snow was dry and powdery and hare-tracks in the snow," but went rather to smoke-filled cafés and dark rooms in the night (p. 13). The tension between these two kinds of space dominates Frederic's imagination. Initially he shies away from images of outer space, investing them with loneliness and fear, and he embraces images of inner space, investing them with an aura of security. The images of inner space are initially developed against the background of a hostile outer world. Early in the novel Frederic moves back and forth between the mountains, where the fighting is and where the forest is gone and there are only "stumps and the broken trunks and the ground torn up" and where the remnants of the trees project, isolated against a background of snow, and the town, with "trees around the square and the long avenue of trees that led to the square," where he sits looking out the window, drinking and watching the snow falling (p. 6). This image of Frederic Henry inside, warm, dry, and secure, watching the world outside struggle against the cold and the wet, recurs in the novel. It is this kind of inner space he seeks in Catherine, loving as he does to let her hair fall over him like a tent and focusing always on every room they inhabit and how they make it a "home." When Frederic arrives at the hospital in Milan, it is, significantly, empty. There is nobody in it, no patients, seemingly no staff, no sheets on the bed, and no room of one's own. By the time he leaves, the hospital has become a home from which he is ejected into the outer world of the war. The apotheosis of his creation of inner space with Catherine is, of course, their rooms in the house in the Swiss mountains, with the big stove in the corner and the feather bed for the lovely dark nights and the air crisp and cold to define for them the security of being inside, snuggled and warm.

But while this archetypal image evokes feelings of warmth and security, it evokes feelings of vulnerability too, for the inner space so carefully and elaborately created is continually threatened by intrusions from the hostile, infinitely larger, outer world; it is but a momentary stay against the confusion of crowded troop trains, where you spend the night on the floor with people walking over you, and of stalled retreats where, like a sitting duck, you wait to be picked off by planes coming in from Austria. It can at any moment be changed to outer space: "But after I had got them out and shut the door and turned off the light it wasn't any good. It was like saying good-by to a statue. After a while I went out and left the hospital and walked back to the hotel in the rain" (p. 332). The vulnerability of inner space is dramatized when Frederic and Catherine, on their way to the station for his departure to the front, encounter a soldier and his girl standing up against a wet stone buttress, his cape pulled around them both to ward off the mist and cold. It is a posture which they consciously or unconsciously imitate a few moments later in sympathetic appreciation of their equal vulnerability. It is pathetic or ironic, or both, that Catherine, driven away in a carriage, her face lighted up in the window, motions Frederic to get back in under the archway and out of the rain.

The threat to inner space, however, comes not only from outside but from inside, from its very nature. When Frederic is retreating from the retreat and trying to get back to Milan, he hops a train and dives in under the canvas of a flatcar, where he is out of sight, secure, warm, dry. But in the process he hits his head against something hard and discovers, on feeling about, that he is sharing this inner space with a gun. The connection of inner space with death is elaborated through Catherine. Carrying an embryo secure, warm, and nourished, her womb is an obvious analogue for the world Frederic creates with her. But at the end of the novel Catherine's womb becomes a chamber of horrors filled with blood and death. In an ironic reversal of expectations, the real danger to Frederic Henry turns out to be not the world of war, the outer world that is so obviously threatening, but the world of love, the inner world that seems overtly so secure.

V

The obvious contradictions of Catherine's character elicit from the critics a bemused perplexity. Jay Gellens' treatment in the introduction to *Twentieth Century Interpretations of "A Farewell to Arms"* is representative:

> . . . she is easy but, somehow, irrevocably pure; has the strength of Beowulf, yet falls apart in a hotel room at the reflection that she is behaving like a whore; is gentle as a deer, and still, in the boat on the way to Switzerland, muses rather crudely about the advantages of being poked "in the tummy" by Henry's oar. . . . Though Catherine is, admittedly, a pleasant, tough little companion, a version of the

woman as partner, it is obvious that if she lacked such courage and resource she could hardly have survived at all in a
world at war. She is, however, feminine enough on her first
night with Henry in the hotel room to feel ashamed, somehow derelict, a tramp. Still, the reader suspects the efficient,
businesslike detachment with which she rigs her schedule at
the hospital to enable the sex with Henry. Yet again, the
very fact of her pregnancy guarantees, in its careless aban-
don, the sincere intensity of the love affair. Further, though
she continually whines about seeing Henry dead in the rain,
and though she naïvely makes her token bet at the race-
track, she can also, during the boat trip, resent her unpro-
pitious maternity. She is, finally, a girl who, at the point of
death, pleads with Henry not to "do our things with another
girl, or say the same things. . . ." Her complexity crystallizes
at last, for the woman she is yearns for the reassurance, yet
only the frank, open, tough little partner would have the
audacity to demand it.[11]

The passage reveals the critics' need to resolve the range of
contradictions in Catherine's character and to make of her
a coherent whole. Catherine has always made the critics
uneasy. Their need to explain her suggests that to accept
and confront her contradictions might be to discover
something rather unpleasant in Hemingway's handling of
women. In fact, Catherine's contradictions are *not* resolv-
able, because her character is determined by forces outside
her; it is a reflection of male psychology and male fantasy
life and is understandable only when seen as a series of
responses to the needs of the male world that surrounds
her. Like Georgiana in "The Birthmark," Catherine
exemplifies the point that female characterization is often
of a different order than male characterization and requires for its analysis different constructs. Carlos Baker
points the way to this distinction as he brings his discussion
of Hemingway's female characters to a conclusion, explaining that "his women are truly emancipated only
through an idea or ideal of service. His heroines, to make

the statement exactly, are meant to show a symbolic or ritualistic function in the service of the artist and the service of man."[12] For every critic, however, who sees in Catherine an ideal, of service or love or whatever, there is another who is ready to attack her. Yet if Catherine's character is a reflection and result of the men around her, then to attack her is absurd. In blaming Catherine for what is Frederic's problem, the critics simply repeat the action of the novel, in which Catherine is the scapegoat whose ritual death allows the hero to survive. Indeed, the critical animus against Catherine is the logical extension of the hostility toward her that is at the heart of *A Farewell to Arms*. The best way to approach the "complexity" of Catherine's character is to see her as one more in a series of cryptograms whose decoding reveals the essential hostility toward women that lies behind this classic love story.

Catherine defines herself in terms of men. Initially we learn that she is a nurse not because of any interest in nursing or even in the concept of service it represents, but because her lover has joined the army and she has a romantic image of his being brought, wounded, to the hospital where she is working. Nursing for Catherine is a way to be with her man when he is at war. And it has the same function in her affair with Frederic when her "silly idea" essentially comes true as she gets herself transferred to the hospital where Frederic has been sent for surgery and recuperation.

Catherine does not determine her own identity. Her sense of self comes from outside, and her self-image is a result of internalizing male attitudes. This self-image is consistently negative. Catherine is pervaded by a self-contempt that affects everything she says and does. When we first meet her, she is berating herself for having failed her first lover: "I was a fool. . . . I didn't know about anything then" (p. 19). When she arrives at the hospital to be with Frederic and he falls in love with her, she reveals a massive craving for reassurance: "I'm afraid I'm not very good at it yet. . . . I'm good. Aren't I good? . . . You see? I'm good. I do what you want" (p. 106). When she discovers she is pregnant, her need for reassurance escalates, because she knows that now she has been really bad: "'You're pretty wonderful.' 'No I'm not. But you musn't mind, darling, I'll try and not make trouble for you. I know I've made trouble now. But haven't I been a good girl until now?'" (p. 138). As her pregnancy advances she feels ugly; she doesn't want Frederic to see her naked and she won't think of getting married until she is slim and attractive again. Feeling inadequate as a lover, she is certain Frederic must be bored, alone with her in a cabin in the mountains. When she finally is dying, she can view that event only in terms of how she is failing him.

Catherine's negative self-image, her self-hatred, and her guilt, are also revealed through her talent for punishing herself. In one of the few conversations she has with Frederic, she chooses a topic guaranteed to give her pain, and she chooses to cast it in a form that is particularly insulting to her: "'Tell me. How many people have you ever loved? . . . You're lying to me. . . . It's all right. Keep right on lying to me. That's what I want you to do'" (pp. 104-105). But Catherine's reason for wanting the information she refuses is just as significant as her request for deception. She wants Frederic to tell her what whores do and don't do so that she can both imitate and transcend them and be in effect a super-whore. Proving Rinaldi's thesis, Catherine Barkley, the lovely English goddess, sees herself as a whore, and what she reveals to Frederic in the gaudy hotel room as he is about to return to the front strikes closer to home than either of them cares to admit. Catherine's situation at this moment is the logical result of Rinaldi's little paradigm. She has picked up the signals of a culture which expects her at once to be "easy" and "irrevocably pure" and will damn her for being either or both.

It is clear that Catherine views herself through the lens of her sexual relation to men and that, when she asks Frederic whether or not she is good, she means good sexually. And it is equally clear that Catherine's attitudes toward her sexuality are as depressing as everything else about her. Speaking to Frederic about the death of her first lover, she remarks: "'You see, I didn't care about the other thing and he could have had it all. He could have had anything he wanted if I would have known. I would have married him or anything'" (p. 19). One is struck by the impersonality of her language; in her eyes her sex is an "it" which her lover could have "had" if she had known he was going to die. Catherine sees her sexuality not as something meaningful or pleasurable for her, but as something separate from herself, a commodity that happens by chance to be hers and that she can use to gain other things, like the approval of men and their involvement with her. Yet, despite the fact that Catherine is sexual not for herself but only for men, she nevertheless expresses a continual sense of sexual failure and a continual need to punish herself for that failure. When she hears of her lover's death, her first impulse is to cut off all her hair, as if this particular form of humiliation were the only appropriate expiation for the crime of not having given "it" to him. And surely, from her point of view, her death in childbirth is fit punishment for having failed Frederic sexually by getting pregnant.

Catherine's attitudes toward her sexuality are an accurate reflection of the sexual nausea that pervades *A Farewell to Arms.* In a world in which the ideal is an asexual priest and in which women are defined solely in sexual terms, it is no wonder Catherine hates herself and feels guilty for existing. While the vision of herself dead in the rain that precedes the announcement of her pregnancy is an obvious instance of foreboding, it has its origins in Catherine's sense of guilt, which projects her death as a form of punishment and retribution. Through her guilt

Catherine registers her appreciation of the hostility toward her of the men through whom she emancipates herself in an "ideal of service"; it is her mode of realizing the undercurrent of hostility that lies behind the protestation of love. As Catherine knows, love for women means you always have to say you're sorry; and she does, again and again and again.

The source of Catherine's compulsive apologizing is revealed in the disparity between the treatment accorded her death and the treatment accorded the deaths of men at war: "'You will not do any such foolishness,' the doctor said. 'You would not die and leave your husband'"; "'You are not going to die. You must not be silly'" (pp. 319, 331). The tone here is only half joking; beneath the jocular surface is a reprimand appropriate to a parent addressing a recalcitrant child. Catherine internalizes the attitude of the doctor and presents that *reductio ad absurdum* of the female experience: she feels guilty for dying and apologizes to the doctor for taking up his valuable time with her death— "I'm sorry I go on so long." Though the two major attendants on her death are male, no shadow of blame falls on them. Catherine never questions Frederic's responsibility for her situation; she seems to operate on the tacit assumption that conception, like contraception, is her doing. And while Frederic is quick to suspect incompetence when it comes to his leg, no doubts are raised about the doctor who performs the Caesarean on Catherine, though usually the need for such an operation is noticed before the child has strangled.* Rather, the responsibility for both her death and the child's is implicitly placed on Catherine. In

---

*This absence of questioning underscores the inevitability of Catherine's death. And this inevitability in turn emphasizes the sense of its being planned from the start, of its being not accident but necessity. In Frederic's case it is clear that things could go right and they could go wrong, and Frederic is alert enough and assertive enough to see that they go right. In Catherine's case not only is she not in control of the outcome but there is no suggestion that the outcome could be different.

contrast, the soldier who hemorrhages to death in the ambulance sling above Frederic Henry does not see himself as stupid, bad, or irresponsible. Even more incongruous is the idea of a doctor referring to a dying soldier in such terms. Indeed, when Miss Van Campen accuses Frederic of the irresponsibility of self-induced jaundice, the results are quite different from those of the comparable scene between Catherine and her doctor. A soldier's responsibility is to himself, but a woman is responsible even in the moment of her death to men. If we weep reading the book at the death of soldiers, we are weeping for the tragic and senseless waste of their lives; we are weeping for them. If we weep at the end of the book, however, it is not for Catherine but for Frederic Henry. All our tears are ultimately for men, because in the world of *A Farewell to Arms* male life is what counts. And the message to women reading this classic love story and experiencing its image of the female ideal is clear and simple: the only good woman is a dead one, and even then there are questions.

THREE

THE GREAT GATSBY
Fitzgerald's *droit de seigneur*

I

The Great Gatsby is another American "love" story centered in hostility to women and the concomitant strategy of the scapegoat. Though at the novel's end the male protagonist is dead, this does not mean that he bears the burden of Catherine or performs the function of scapegoat or is the object of the novel's animus. Reversal of roles does not mean reversal of emotions or symbolic value. It simply means that a different pattern can make the same point.[1] Not dead Gatsby but surviving Daisy is the object of the novel's hostility and its scapegoat. And the vision of love as war, implicit in *A Farewell to Arms*, is here played out as a struggle for power in an elaborate pattern of advantage and disadvantage in which romance is finally but a strategy for male victory.

In *A Farewell to Arms*, the idealization of romantic love covers and disguises hostility; in *The Great Gatsby*, the two emotions coexist and are coequal. Like most of F. Scott Fitzgerald's work, *The Great Gatsby* is spun out upon the twin emotional impulses of romanticism and moral indignation. But unlike his earlier fiction, *The Great Gatsby* presents a complex vision of the interrelation between the two impulses, and its final meaning resides in an understanding of the nature of that relationship. That women are the focus of both emotions is a primary key to this understanding. In the archetypal American experience of romantic nostalgia, in which the sense of wonder is intimately and instantly coupled with the sense of loss, women are the symbolic counters. It is hardly irrelevant that the Carraway/Fitzgerald vision of a lost America is so clearly linked to Gatsby's vision of Daisy, for in the male mind, which is at once Gatsby, Carraway, and Fitzgerald, the impulse to wonder is instinctively associated with the image of woman, and the ensuing gambits of the romantic imagination are played out in female metaphors. In this fable of the New World in which Gatsby is the incarnation of the American dreamer and his history is the history of the "American dream," it is Daisy herself who is America, the "fresh green breast of the new world."

In "Elegie XIX," John Donne invokes the sense of wonder associated with the discovery of America ("O my America! my newfound land") to describe his emotion on seeing his mistress at her moment of "full nakedness"; in *The Great Gatsby* Fitzgerald reverses the process and by close scrutiny of his mistress reveals America to be a bitch whose green breast "once pandered in whispers to the last and greatest of all human dreams." Both the sense of wonder and the sense of loss are associated with women, and women are the object of the novel's moral indignation just as they are the object of its romanticism. Thus, the pattern which best defines the central action of *The Great Gatsby* is that of investment/divestment, through which the golden girl is revealed to be a common weed and the fresh green breast of the new world turns pander to men's dreams, feeding them not on the milk of wonder but on the foul dust of bootleg liquor.

II

Gatsby's imaginative investment in Daisy is evident in his description of her as "the first 'nice' girl he had ever known" (*The Great Gatsby* [1925; rpt. New York: Scribners, 1953], p. 148). The quotation marks around "nice" indicate that the word is being used not as a reference to personality but as an index to social status and that Jay Gatsby's interest in Daisy Fay lies in what she represents rather than in what she is. She is for him symbolic rather than personal: he later remarks to Nick that Daisy's relation to Tom was "in any case . . . just personal" (p. 152). Gatsby's relation to Daisy is quite impersonal:

> He went to her house, at first with other officers from Camp Taylor, then alone. It amazed him—he had never been in such a beautiful house before. But what gave it an air of breathless intensity was that Daisy lived there—it was as casual a thing to her as his tent out at camp was to him. There was a ripe mystery about it, a hint of bedrooms upstairs more beautiful and cool than other bedrooms, of gay and radiant activities taking place through its corridors, and of romances that were not musty and laid away already in lavender, but fresh and breathing and redolent of this year's shining motor-cars and of dances whose flowers were scarcely withered. (p. 148)

Gatsby thinks of Daisy in relation to the objects that surround her. Indeed, he cannot separate his vision of her from his vision of the house in which she lives, for the house gains its "air of breathless intensity" not from the fact that *Daisy* lives there but from the fact that she *lives* there. That Daisy is so at home in this rich world from which he is excluded overwhelms Gatsby. She becomes identified in his mind with that house and that world, and they, in turn, represent for him a life of romantic possibility commensurate with his wild imaginings. Daisy is for Gatsby the house of romance which he can only enter through her.

But Daisy does not simply represent or incarnate that magical world Gatsby desires; she is herself the ultimate object in it. It is she for whom men compete, and possessing her is the clearest sign that one has made it into that magical world. Gatsby's desire for Daisy is enhanced by the fact that she is the object of the desires of so many other men: "It excited him, too, that many men had already loved Daisy—it increased her value in his eyes" (p. 148). Their desire ratifies his sense of her symbolic significance. That Daisy is the most expensive item on the market is a point Tom makes when he gives her on the night before they are married a string of pearls valued at $350,000. Daisy is that which money exists to buy; her presence both indicates the fact of money and gives point to its possession. Having her makes Tom Buchanan's house in East Egg finished and "right"; not having her makes Gatsby's mansion in West Egg incomplete and "wrong." It is not surprising, then, that Daisy's meaning should crystallize for Gatsby, and for Nick, around the perception that her voice is full of money. One can only wonder that it took them so long to formulate the obvious.

But money is never just money to the imagination that made a fetish of being rich: "that was the inexhaustible charm that rose and fell in it, the jingle of it, the cymbals' song of it. . . . High in a white palace the king's daughter, the golden girl" (p. 120). Money is coin of the realm of romance, and the golden girl is valued not just because she provides access to the king's palace or because she is expensive. She is valued as well for the connotations that shimmer in the words "high" and "white"—a rarefied kingdom, pure and free, where the imagination reigns unsullied by the ashy wasteland of the real world and romps like the mind of God. The high white palace is an analogue for Gatsby's "secret place above the trees," from which he can look down on the world and "suck on the pap of life, gulp down the incomparable milk of wonder"; and Daisy herself becomes, as the metaphors suggest, the symbol of the possibilities for wonder that his imagination creates (p. 112).

The pervasive spatial metaphor, however, reveals another aspect of the golden girl crucial to her hold on the impersonality of the romantic imagination. She is hard to get; she has to be worked for, dragons must be fought, castles penetrated, and walls scaled. And the harder she is to get the more she is valued, because the quest for and possession of her gives the pink-suited knight his identity. When Gatsby weds "his unutterable visions" to Daisy's "perishable breath" and makes her his holy grail, she becomes the organizing point of his existence, providing him with a structure that determines what he will do and who he will be. She becomes his access to a certain self-image: "he wanted to recover something, some idea of himself perhaps, that had gone into loving Daisy" (p. 111). It is through Daisy that Gatsby acquires the image of himself as the faithful unto death, the one for whom time and change mean nothing, whose love is a pure flame that feeds upon and fires itself. It is through her that he realizes himself in the posture of the dedicated lover who reads a Chicago newspaper for five years in the hope simply of catching a glimpse of her name. It is for her that he accomplishes the heroic feat of making himself into a millionaire, and it is for her that he builds his palace in West Egg.

This investment of self in Daisy means, of course, that Gatsby needs Daisy to validate him. Since everything is done for her, she must be worthy of this investment in her and she must provide a response commensurate to it. The ritual of validation is the last of the symbolic functions Daisy performs for Gatsby. Gatsby will have his great reunion with Daisy only at his house or, if that is impossible, then next door to it, for he does not wish to see *her* but rather for her to see what he has done *for* her, as if only through her eyes will his vision of himself be made real. The same implicit demand is there when he spills out before her his wealth of gorgeous shirts: they are deployed to exact tribute from her. It is no wonder that Daisy cries. What response could possibly be adequate to this demonstration? Her tears are an understandable reaction at once to the pathos in the demonstration and to the pressure on her to be valuable enough to validate the identity so painfully set before her.

But it is impossible for anyone to be this valuable, and so Daisy is inevitably inadequate to Gatsby's vision. Daisy can't help but fail Gatsby, because such failure is inherent in the terms of his quest; or, to put it in terms of the pattern I am developing, the investment of the romantic imagination is prelude to the divestment of moral indignation because the one creates the conditions for the other. Gatsby's "unutterable visions" have, after all, been quite consciously wed to Daisy's "perishable breath." The disparity between object and investment could hardly be more obvious. Thus, possession of Daisy is necessarily accompanied by a sense of diminishment:

> As I went over to say good-by I saw that the expression of bewilderment had come back into Gatsby's face, as though a faint doubt had occurred to him as to the quality of his present happiness. Almost five years: There must have been moments even that afternoon when Daisy tumbled short of his dreams—not through her own fault, but because of the colossal vitality of his illusion. It had gone beyond her, beyond everything. He had thrown himself into it with a creative passion, adding to it all the time, decking it out with every bright feather that drifted his way. No amount of fire or freshness can challenge what a man will store up in his ghostly heart.   (p. 97)

In its analysis of the romantic imagination, *The Great Gatsby* reveals that the romantic potential of any object depends on its inaccessibility (surely the fact that Gatsby has made his fortune from prohibition is one of the most brilliant touches of the novel). Gatsby's parties seen from Nick's cottage are one thing and Gatsby's parties when one is at them are another; inside, Myrtle's apartment is sordid chaos, but outside, looking up, the light in her window suggests "the inexhaustible variety of life"; Daisy viewed from the outside as an object to be possessed is one thing and Daisy confronted as a person is quite another, for desire depends on impediment. Indeed, Daisy has symbolic power precisely because she suggests that which cannot be possessed at the same time that she excites so intensely the desire to possess. Redolent of yesterdays and tomorrows but never of todays, her voice exudes a "promise that she has done gay, exciting things just a while since and that there were gay, exciting things hovering in the next hour" (pp. 9-10). When confronted with the present, she can only cry petulantly, "What do people plan?" and "I always watch for the longest day in the year and then miss it" (p. 12). As a creature of the present, Daisy is nothing, for Daisy possessed is Daisy lost.

In a letter to Edmund Wilson about *The Great Gatsby*, Fitzgerald described the "BIG FAULT" in the book: "I gave no account (and had no feeling about or knowledge of) the emotional relations between Gatsby and Daisy from the time of their reunion to the catastrophe."[2] But surely, far from being a fault, this omission defines the meaning of the novel—that meaning which a little later in the same letter the author says has eluded most of the novel's readers. For the truth of the matter is that nothing is less relevant to this love story than the details of the relationship between Daisy and Gatsby. There are no emotional relations between them to give an account of; there is only an emotional relation between Gatsby and his "unutterable visions," of which Daisy is the unwitting symbol who comes into existence only at the moment when his lips' touch creates her as the incarnation of himself. And in this story, which is preeminently the fable of a past that is a future and a future that is a past, nothing could be farther from its point than an attempt to document a present. Its concern is with the experience of longing and the sense of loss—a romantic readiness for the future and a romantic nostalgia for the past.

III

The pattern of investment/divestment that dominates the structure of *The Great Gatsby* is invoked by the language Nick chooses to imagine Gatsby's last moments alive: "He must have looked up at an unfamiliar sky through frightening leaves and shivered as he found what a grotesque thing a rose is" (p. 162). Investment makes divestment inevitable. The escalation of expectations brings in its wake an exacerbated sense of failure, and a rose becomes grotesque because one has expected it to be more than a flower. At the heart of the romantic imagination is the need for a sense of loss. In order to understand this particular necessity of loss, we must examine the other major pattern in the book: advantage/disadvantage and its concomitant questions of power. *The Great Gatsby* is a book about power, and the romantic investment and indignant divestment of women is an aspect of and mask for the struggle for power between men which is its subject.

Gatsby has an immense need to "serve." His representative posture is that of the host, gliding imperceptibly and bountifully among guests who cannot even thank him because most of them don't know who he is. Such a disparity between giving and getting is worth focusing on. While Gatsby may give his parties in the hopes that Daisy or someone who knows her will drop in, the role of host is central to his personality. Gatsby operates from a need to placate, a need to make sure that no one has a grudge against him, and that he never owes anybody anything. When an unknown woman tears her dress at one of his parties, she receives "inside of a week" a package with a new evening gown in it. When Nick arranges the meeting with Daisy, he is offered in return for this minor service the possibility of a fortune. When one of the women at one of his parties says, "he doesn't want any trouble with *any-body*," she has put her finger on Gatsby. What he wants is the image of the perfect host, bidding farewell to satisfied guests from the top of his stairs in magnificent isolation.

Behind this need to assume the posture of the world's servant, the magnificent giver who is above and beyond the need for service in return, is Gatsby's conviction that in spite of his wealth he is tolerated in the world of Toms and Daisys by a grace for which he can compensate only by an excess of service. His definition of himself, after all, is that of the interloper par excellence who took Daisy "because he had no real right to touch her hand" (p. 149). When Gatsby firsts meets Daisy, his position in relation to her is one of disadvantage, and his romantic investment in her grows out of his perception of himself as the excluded outsider and his vision of her as the privileged insider: "She was the first 'nice' girl he had ever known. In various unrevealed capacities he had come in contact with such people, but always with indiscernible barbed wire between" (p. 148). Daisy represents for Gatsby an ultimate position of advantage: "[He] was overwhelmingly aware of . . . Daisy, gleaming like silver, safe and proud above the hot struggles of the poor" (p. 150).[3]

The sense of disadvantage, of being outside the rich house and the rich life into which the rich girl has vanished and of realizing the need to get that rich girl if one is going to get that house and that life, has, however, undercurrents of hostility. Yet this hostility never surfaces in Gatsby. It is Nick who registers the emotions implicit in Gatsby's experience and psychology that Gatsby himself could not express without losing the unself-consciousness which saves him from the moral indictment consuming the rest of his world. The strategic brilliance of *The Great Gatsby* lies in this division of the psychological action of investment/ divestment between Gatsby and Nick. It is this strategy that allows Fitzgerald to eat his cake and have it too.

Nick and Gatsby are, of course, not opposites but analogues; the similarities between them are insistent enough to make us aware of their shared identity. Central here is their mutual need to appear at an advantage behind which lies a shared sense of disadvantage. The importance for Nick of appearing at an advantage is seen in the way he chooses to begin his narrative. Nick immediately explains to us that he is tolerant because of some advice his father once gave him: " 'Whenever you feel like criticizing anyone,' he told me, 'just remember that all the people in this world haven't had the advantages that you've had.'" While his father's advice seems to open up areas of tolerance for those who are less advantaged, it also provides Nick with the rationale for immense anger at those who seem more advantaged. And as we soon begin to doubt Nick's tolerance, so we begin to suspect his initial self-presentation and to discover that, like Gatsby, his true sense of himself is that of the disadvantaged outsider. This is surely one of the meanings of Nick's statement that his has been a story of the West—of people not at home, relating to a world whose codes and structures they don't understand.[4] But even within this group of Westerners, all of whom are at some disadvantage in the East, Nick seems to feel uniquely disadvantaged. His social awkwardness is apparent in the twelve lemon cakes he provides for Gatsby's reunion and in the queer behavior of the old Finn he employs to assist him—a striking contrast to the grace and elegance of Daisy's home, complete with butler, where Nick confesses, "You make me feel uncivilized, Daisy" (p.

13). In the midst of potentially explosive situations it is Nick who feels the awkwardness and who tries to maintain the patina of convention in defiance of the raw emotions around him. Indeed, in almost every instance of social interaction, Nick appears to be awkward, out of place, and uncomfortable.

The connection between Nick's sense of disadvantage and his identification with Gatsby is made explicit at one point in the book. In explaining the reasons for his not having seen Gatsby for a period of time during the summer, he says, "Mostly I was in New York, trotting around with Jordan and trying to ingratiate myself with her senile aunt—but finally I went over to his house one Sunday afternoon" (p. 102). Nick then describes the scene which took place that afternoon when a casual attendant at one of Gatsby's parties brought Tom Buchanan in for a drink. The point of Nick's account is to record at once Gatsby's touching "readiness," the rudeness of Tom and his friends, and his own sense of outrage at Gatsby's humiliation. Nick's fierceness is the result of identification with Gatsby, for Gatsby, of course, does not know that anything has happened. But Nick can't stand the idea that Mrs. Sloane, despite her invitation, doesn't really want Gatsby to come to dinner, because he can't stand the idea of himself trotting after Jordan. Thus, in taking on the stance of Gatsby's defender against the insults of the world ("I'll get somebody for you, Gatsby. Don't worry. Just trust me and I'll get somebody for you"), Nick is symbolically seeking to avenge his own sense of insult and to adjust the balance of power a little.

What is striking about the scene discussed above is its conjunction so seemingly casual (but this is a book which depends considerably on a series of seemingly casual conjunctions) of Gatsby's humiliation and Nick's relation to Jordan. The nature of the connection that *The Great Gatsby* reveals between a male sense of disadvantage and attitudes toward women is perhaps best understood if we examine a comment Fitzgerald made in recording the profound effect on him of being a poor boy trying to win his rich girl, Zelda: "I have never been able to stop wondering where my friends' money came from, nor to stop thinking that at one time a sort of *droit de seigneur* might have been exercised to give one of them my girl."[5] The burden of this comment is the poor boy's powerlessness, and this powerlessness is registered most clearly through the disposal of his girl. When men invest women with the significance of ultimate possessions, they make them the prime counters in their power games with each other. Thus, women, who have themselves no actual power, become symbolic of the power of moneyed men; and while the real enemy in the passage above is the writer's "friends," it is the girl who becomes the repository for the animus of the disadvantaged male.

The epigraph for *The Great Gatsby* provides an image of the connection between the structures of romantic love and the question of power:

Then wear the gold hat, if that will move her;
   If you can bounce high, bounce for her too,
Till she cry "Lover, gold-hatted, high-bouncing lover,
   I must have you!"

The drama here is a drama of power, and the lesson is how to move one's self into a position of advantage. It is a lesson Nick learns well and it provides the pattern for much of his behavior. Implicit in the epigraph is the point that women only *appear* to be immovable, non-appetitive; they only appear to have the advantage. In fact, they can be made to cry and to reveal a driving appetitive necessity if one is willing to play the gold-hatted lover. Even if the part is sometimes that of a fool, decorated and gyrating, who trots around and ingratiates himself, it is worth it because the result is a resounding advantage. While Gatsby plays the part of the gold-hatted lover, Nick articulates why and plays out the power game to its predestined conclusion.

In one of the early scenes in the book, when Nick comes to East Egg to visit Tom and Daisy, we are given a demonstration of how Nick operates to make her cry. Tom's possession of Daisy is used as the keynote in his effort to impress Nick with his status. The description of her echoes and interweaves with the description of her setting, signaling her position as the ultimate furnishing in Tom Buchanan's establishment. The scene on which Nick enters is meant to exact an emotional tribute from him, and he reacts to it accordingly, standing motionless until its orchestrator comes in and shuts the windows with a boom. Daisy's remark about being paralyzed with happiness is ironic in light of the actual situation; it is Nick who is paralyzed and at a disadvantage in the presence of the mock paralysis, the mask of immobility that Daisy puts on as her part in the effort to exact tribute from him: "indeed, I was almost surprised into murmuring an apology for having disturbed her by coming in" (p. 9). One might describe the rest of the scene as Nick's revenge for having been placed in this position.

Shortly after Tom brings the balloons down to earth by shutting the window, Daisy breaks her paralysis long enough to murmur to Nick the name of her guest. Paying tribute, as he is obviously asked to do, to the magic of Daisy's voice, Nick nevertheless feels compelled to mention, although in parentheses, that "I've heard it said that Daisy's murmur was only to make people lean toward her; an irrelevant criticism that made it no less charming" (p. 9). But, of course, the criticism is not irrelevant or Nick wouldn't mention it, and indeed it does make Daisy less charming for it implies that the quality of her voice is simply something put on in order to gain an advantage over others.

At dinner Jordan and Daisy "talked . . . with a bantering inconsequence that was never quite chatter, that was as cool as their white dresses and their impersonal eyes in the absence of all desire. They were here, and they accepted Tom and me, making only a polite pleasant effort to entertain or to be entertained" (pp. 12-13). But this disinterest, this cool superiority in the presence of men is only an appearance. A moment after Nick makes this observation the phone rings, bringing the ugly intrusion of Tom's mistress into the apparent order of Daisy's life and dislodging her at once from her table and her pose. Then Jordan, who could barely turn her head to acknowledge Nick's presence, is suddenly alert; she sits up, telling Nick to be quiet as she leans forward to hear what is happening. Immobility is revealed as pose and the pose as power politics.

After dinner Nick has a *tete à tete* with Daisy on the porch. In this confessional scene Nick is cast in the role of sympathetic listener, while Daisy speaks of her past with Tom. But at the precise moment when Nick is in danger of being moved by Daisy's account of her suffering, "her voice broke off, ceasing to compel my attention, my belief" (p. 18). Uneasy, he looks up, and, sure enough, he discovers in the "absolute smirk on her lovely face" that it has all been "a trick of some sort to exact a contributary emotion from me" (p. 18). The effect of this elaborate unmasking of Daisy is to discount her reliability as an interpreter of her own experience and to ensure that she will have no claims on our sympathy. Her suffering is reduced to a pose, and her vision of what it means to be born female is defined as a gimmick to exact tribute. Daisy may cry over Gatsby's shirts but Nick has seen to it that no tears will be shed over her.

Nick's divesting mentality operates on Daisy's invested image to expose her for what she "really" is—common, as her name implies. Very carefully, he removes the petals that constitute her allure until there is nothing left but a denuded center. The terms Nick uses to describe Daisy insist on her essential nothingness. Like the frosted wedding-cake ceiling under which she is first discovered, Daisy's talk is chatter, banter, sugared air. Nick makes quite clear that one never *listens* to what Daisy says. Like her face, her voice is disembodied and in Nick's eyes she always flutters. Analogously, she is for Nick asexual. Gatsby is not the only one who is surprised by the appearance of her child. Thus, what for the investing imagination is a central ingredient in its obsession—the whiteness of the golden girl, her lack of physical substance, her ability to project herself entirely as image—becomes for the divesting eye a central source of its indictment. Purity becomes asexuality becomes sterility, and Daisy is revealed to be the true inhabitant of the wasteland whose casual act of murder rips open the breast of possibility in the new world. When Gatsby weds his visions to her image, it is but a prelude, like the "Wedding March" overheard in the hotel on that fateful afternoon, to sterility and death. And when Nick returns to West Egg after his evening with Tom and Daisy to discover Gatsby stretching out his arms toward the green light at the end of her dock, one can feel only irony, pity, and perhaps even horror at the fact that the object of such adoration is Daisy Fay Buchanan. If we wish an iconographic tool for comprehending the dual impulses that play upon Daisy in *The Great Gatsby* and form its major psychological action, we need only compare our first view of her with our last: from the high hall, the rosy-colored and fragile room where she dominates as the ultimate ornament, the incarnation of men's dreams, she descends to the kitchen pantry, where she sits with Tom in conspiratorial silence over a plate of cold chicken and a bottle of ale. She has indeed become the foul dust that floats in Gatsby's wake.

IV

Nick's relation to Jordan is a less complex version of his relation to Daisy. Although Jordan is of the same class as Daisy and has the same image-making potential ("I knew now why her face was familiar—its pleasing contemptuous expression had looked out at me from many rotogravure pictures of the sporting life at Asheville and Hot Springs and Palm Beach" [p. 19]), Nick never invests Jordan as Gatsby invests Daisy. Thus, the focus of Nick's relation to Jordan is on that part of romance which is divestment. And, concomitantly, the power struggle of advantage/ disadvantage that lies behind the need to divest predominates so that Nick's interaction with Jordan is structured almost entirely in terms of power.

Throughout a major part of their relationship, Nick's position in relation to Jordan can be defined as one of disadvantage. The disastrous first encounter, when he feels himself on the verge of apologizing to her for existing, is followed by Nick's attendance at Gatsby's party, where Jordan "saves" him from a situation so uncomfortable that he has decided the only way out is to get hopelessly drunk. The status Jordan provides for him at the party persists when he begins to go around with her and is "flattered" because everyone knows her name. Then later he confesses that she is security for him—she makes the decade of his thirties look less lonely. Nick is understandably rather vague in trying to define his feelings for Jordan; they do not bear much looking into. From that first moment, when her example of "complete self-sufficiency draws a stunned tribute" from him, he has resisted the paying of that tribute, has resented her advantage over him, and has sought to destroy her pose. Later in the evening that he first meets Jordan, he quite consciously plants the hint, just as he did with Daisy, that there is something wrong with her: "I had heard some story of her

too, a critical, unpleasant story, but what it was I had for-
gotten long ago" (p. 19). Again, Nick's air of casualness, of
a tolerance immune to unpleasant innuendoes, should not
mislead us. When he finally discovers what is wrong with
Jordan, it proves to be, despite his assurances to the contrary, of the utmost importance:

> The bored haughty face that she turned to the world con-
> cealed something—most affectations conceal something
> eventually, even though they don't in the beginning—and
> one day I found what it was. . . . Jordan Baker instinctively
> avoided clever, shrewd men, and now I saw that this was
> because she felt safer on a plane where any divergence from
> a code would be thought impossible. She was incurably dis-
> honest. She wasn't able to endure being at a disadvantage
> and, given this unwillingness, I suppose she had begun deal-
> ing in subterfuges when she was very young in order to
> keep that cool, insolent smile turned to the world and yet
> satisfy the demands of her hard, jaunty body. (pp. 58-59)

This analysis of Jordan's character works well in Nick's
design of divesting Jordan's image of its potency and of
establishing an advantage in relation to her. First, there is
the revelation, as with Daisy, that Jordan's image of cool
superiority, immovable impersonality is a façade, an affectation designed to cover ravenous needs and the appeti-
tiveness of her hard, jaunty body. Then there is the even
more important revelation that this façade has been constructed because Jordan is unable to endure being at a
disadvantage. Thus the source of the image which constitutes Jordan's advantage in relation to Nick is revealed to
be a sense of disadvantage so massive that she lies
pathologically in order to maintain it.

But Nick does not stop his process of divestment here,
for he chooses to follow up his "analysis" of Jordan's character by referring to an incident that, unless one understands Nick's motive, seems totally irrelevant to what has

gone before: "It was on the same house-party that we had a curious conversation about driving a car. It started because she passed so close to some workmen that our fender flicked a button on one man's coat" (p. 59). Given the plot of this novel, to reveal that someone is a careless driver is to identify her as a potential murderer. Like Daisy, Jordan is defined as one who uses the status and power symbolized throughout the novel by the image of the automobile for her own needs and pleasures, careless and indifferent to the existence of anyone else. And thus, like Daisy, Jordan takes her place in the foul dust that floats in the wake of Gatsby's death.

Nick's analysis of Jordan reveals, of course, as much, if not more, about him than it does about her, and we are justified if we examine him in the light of his dictum about the function of affectations. For surely Nick's self-deprecation ("Jordan Baker instinctively avoided clever, shrewd men") and his constant air of tolerant casualness are as much an affectation as is Jordan's bored, haughty face. And what Nick's affectation covers is, not too surprisingly, precisely that need which he sees as the source of Jordan's façade. He cannot bear to be at a disadvantage and so he will lie: "It made no difference to me. Dishonesty in a woman is a thing you never blame deeply—I was casually sorry, and then I forgot" (p. 59). But Nick does not forget, and he does blame, and the one place where dishonesty makes a difference to him is in a woman.

Nick's final scene with Jordan is a *tour de force* of the struggle for advantage. In recounting his last meeting with her, Nick divests Jordan's image of any potency it might still have. He remembers thinking that "she looked like a good illustration, her chin raised a little jauntily, her hair the color of an autumn leaf, her face the same brown tint as the fingerless glove on her knee" (p. 178). This description is reminiscent of his initial vision of her, but there is a subtle difference to mark the shift that has occurred in the balance of power between them since then. This time her chin is raised only a *little* jauntily, and she is reduced to the level of a good illustration, a subtle form of devaluation that suggests at once her affectation, her unreality, and her easy classification, and hence dismissal, as a type. When Nick has finished saying what he has to say to put his life in order, Jordan tells him, "without comment," that she is engaged to someone else. Nick immediately doubts her, assuming that she is lying in order to gain an advantage, but he pretends to be surprised; after thinking for a moment that perhaps he has made a mistake in not marrying Jordan, he realizes he has been correct in his assessment of her (hasn't he just had proof of it?) and gets up to say good-bye. At this point, Jordan invokes the inevitable driving metaphor in the hope of gaining a final advantage, only to have it backfire: "'You said a bad driver was only safe until she met another bad driver? Well, I met another bad driver, didn't I? I mean it was careless of me to make such a wrong guess. I thought you were rather an honest, straightforward person. I thought it was your secret pride.' 'I'm thirty,' I said. 'I'm five years too old to lie to myself and call it honor!'" (p. 179). Nick, as always, has the last word, and that last word in this charade of deceptions is the ultimate lie, for Nick implies that out of her sense of disadvantage Jordan stoops to the slander of calling him dishonest. Advantage, Mr. Carraway.

V

The relationship between the pattern of investment/ divestment and that of advantage/disadvantage is in some ways most interestingly demonstrated in Fitzgerald's treatment of Myrtle Wilson. If Jordan is Daisy's parallel, Myrtle is her opposite. Placed in a setting as far as possible

from the realm where Daisy reigns as ultimate ornament—no white palace for her but a set of rooms
above a garage in the middle of the wasteland—Myrtle is
neither a nice girl nor a golden girl. She is cheap, she is
vulgar, she is poor, and she is definitely lower class. Her
coarse voice contains no charming murmurs or magical
promises. No disembodied image floating in a diaphanous
haze of white dresses and shimmering surroundings, she is
fully bodied in her "surplus and sensuous" flesh. If ever
there was an object that resisted idealization, it is Myrtle.
And so she is mistress, not wife; she dresses in blues and
browns, not white; and when she dares to invoke the sacred name of Daisy, she gets her nose smashed.

Yet, at the end Myrtle rises. Her impassioned plunge
toward her own particular green light and her subsequent
death are registered as a "tragic achievement," and she
emerges as a figure of vitality, passion, and reality in the
midst of the wasteland: "The mouth was wide open and
ripped at the corners, as though she had choked a little in
giving up the tremendous vitality she had stored so long"
(p. 138). In a final play on a predominant image, Myrtle
Wilson's coarse and unlovely mouth becomes the symbol
of her achievement, obliterating the bright charm of
Daisy's mouth in an image of loss that may well elicit tears.
The opposition between Myrtle and Daisy is a collision
course, and, when the crash finally happens and the dust
clears, Myrtle is idealized and Daisy is devalued. Daisy is
revealed to be a common flower and Myrtle appropriates
to herself the mythic connotations implied in her name.

The reasons for this reversal, however, are not hard to
find. If the investment/divestment of Daisy is the result of
her relationship to male power, a woman who has no such
relationship will not be subject to the same impulses. Myrtle is finally transcendent because from the beginning she
is powerless and disadvantaged. This is a crucial factor to
consider in analyzing the split between dark and white

"ladies" in our literature and in understanding the ways they have been portrayed. The mystique that often surrounds the dark ladies derives from the fact that they constitute a class of social/sexual/economic outcasts whom men can afford to romanticize and ultimately idealize precisely because they are doomed. It is hardly accidental that Myrtle's elevation occurs at the moment of her death. Nor is it accidental that its source is her sexuality. To elevate woman as sexual object is to elevate woman at her most dependent, derivative, and powerless. In Myrtle's death the metaphoric structures which contain the psychological action of *The Great Gatsby* come full circle, for the fresh green breast of the new world that turns pander to men's dreams turns tragic symbol in the ripped-off breast of Myrtle Wilson.

VI

In 1934, in the process of writing an introduction for the Modern Library edition of *The Great Gatsby*, Fitzgerald reread his novel and reexamined his relationship to it in an effort to define what he had been trying to do and what his book was about. In this reexamination Fitzgerald insisted on the essential honesty of the book: "Reading it over one can see how it could have been improved—yet without feeling guilty of any discrepancy from the truth, as far as I saw it; truth or rather the *equivalent* of the truth, the attempt at honesty of imagination. . . . I think it is an honest book. . . . If there is a clear conscience, a book can survive—at least in one's feelings about it."[6] At the risk of being facile, one might say that such insistence suggests a certain uneasiness on the subject of the novel's truthfulness, and well it might, for the imagination to which *The Great Gatsby* is faithful is in fact deeply dishonest.

One of the major concerns of critical commentary on *The Great Gatsby* has been the attempt to determine whether or not Nick Carraway is a reliable narrator.[7] This question is prompted by certain difficulties in Nick's character and presentation, among which is, to some critics at least, his dishonesty. Yet, the interpretations of those critics who see in Nick's dishonesty the key, either unintentional or intentional, to Nick's unreliability seem misguided. The narrative structure of *The Great Gatsby* is not the result of "careless technique and cloudy thinking";[8] it could be more accurately described as one of Fitzgerald's most self-conscious and most successful solutions to the problem of how to tell a story. Nor is there any internal evidence to support the claim that Fitzgerald intends us to see Nick as unreliable; no alternate narrator is present in the novel to make sense of the shambles which result from questioning Nick's credibility. Yet, Nick is dishonest. How then are we to understand this dishonesty, and how are we to reconcile it with Fitzgerald's control of his material?

It is not irrelevant that most of Gary Scrimgeour's criticism of Nick relates to his treatment of Jordan and Daisy. Scrimgeour indicts Nick for "the final falsehood into which his loyalty to the dead Gatsby forces him," that of concealing the fact that Daisy was the driver of the car which killed Myrtle Wilson.[9] But Nick's deceit derives not simply from his loyalty to the dead Gatsby nor from his desire to avoid trouble; it is equally the product of his assumption that the rich, and rich *women* in particular, are incapable of moral responsibility. He admits to having a different standard of honesty for women than he has for men and thus to being disinclined to attribute moral responsibility to women. To confront Daisy with her crime would be to accord her a stature incompatible with his assessment of her. Nick's behavior in this matter is, however, perfectly normal in a culture which defines women—legally, emotionally, psychologically—as children. Thus, to accuse Nick of dishonesty in his treatment of women and Fitzgerald of carelessness in handling that dishonesty is to miss the point. Nick's dishonesty goes unrecognized by Fitzgerald for the same reasons that it goes unrecognized by most of the novel's readers: it is not perceived as dishonest because it is common, pervasive, and "natural" to a sexist society. *The Great Gatsby* is a dishonest book because the culture from which it derives and which it reflects is radically dishonest.

At the beginning of this chapter I discussed the dual impulses of satire and romanticism in Fitzgerald's work and suggested that *The Great Gatsby* is central to Fitzgerald because it both realizes and solves this ambivalence of style and personality. I submit that Fitzgerald is able to achieve his particular combination of tones by drawing on a large cultural lie which he neither recognizes as such nor makes any conscious commentary upon. It is the existence of a double standard, of one set of responses appropriate to women and another to men, that makes possible Fitzgerald's simultaneous indulgence in and indictment of the romantic imagination.

Nick exemplifies the cultural double standard in that he judges the behavior of men and women quite differently. He blames Jordan for relatively minor dishonesties, yet he accepts Gatsby's massive dishonesties with understanding. Nick would never call Gatsby's detours around the fact of his past dishonesty, for in Nick's eyes Gatsby's behavior is floated clear upon the floodtide of Nick's empathy with its sources. Yet, those sources are hardly different from the sources of Jordan's behavior: both behaviors stem from a sense of disadvantage and both are strategies for gaining an advantage. Nick is also aware that Gatsby is a creature of poses and a master at projecting images of himself calculated to produce a certain effect: "After that I lived like a young rajah in all the capitals of Europe—Paris, Venice, Rome—collecting jewels, chiefly rubies, hunting big game, painting a little, things for myself only, and trying to forget something very sad that had happened to me long ago" (p. 66). Nick does not, however, call Gatsby's "old sport" an affectation nor does he feel the need to discover what his elaborate posture of "correctness" covers. While quick to assure us that he has found the key to Jordan's character in the relationship between her affectation of boredom and her dishonesty, he ignores the cannibalistic implications of Meyer Wolfsheim's cuff links, for Gatsby's character is presumably too complex to be explained by a connection between correctness and cannibalism.

The disparity between Nick's judgment of Daisy and his judgment of Gatsby is of primary importance, for behind this disparity is a radical, if common, form of the pervasive cultural double standard. This form can be summarized as follows: men are legitimate subjects for romantic investment and women are not; men can support it and women cannot; Daisy must fail Gatsby but Gatsby need not fail Nick. This is *the* double standard which produces the disparate judgments in the book; which makes Daisy's narcissism a reason for damning her (Nick is careful to note that Daisy heads for a mirror as soon as they reach their room at the Plaza), yet makes Gatsby's utter solipsism the occasion for a muted romantic overture; which makes Gatsby's exacting of tribute from Daisy as he pours his magnificent heap of shirts before her a heroic affirmation and makes Daisy's attempt to exact tribute from Nick a cheap trick; which excuses Gatsby's crimes as part of his great design, yet damns Daisy utterly as a careless driver. Gatsby's investment in Daisy is seen as a tragic error, the fault, however, not of himself but of that bitch America; while Nick's investment in Gatsby is achieved despite his awareness of what Gatsby represents and is the tribute legitimately due one who "turned out all right at the end." And so we have the absurdity and the dishonesty of Nick romanticizing Gatsby for his heroic though misguided romanticization of

Daisy, who becomes, of course, the excluded middle in the love story of Nick Carraway and Jay Gatsby.

There is, then, a final stage in the pattern of investment/divestment. Gatsby's investment in Daisy is followed by Nick's divestment of her, and that, in turn, is followed by Nick's investment in Gatsby.[10] But this investment is not followed by nor does it seem to require any subsequent process of divestment. What was in the case of Daisy an inevitable consequence of the romantic imagination is in this case evitable, and Gatsby is exempt from the process of disillusion. Fitzgerald accomplishes this duplicity by a sleight of hand of which he was well aware: "Also you are right about Gatsby being blurred and patchy. I never at any one time saw him clear myself—for he started as one man I knew and then changed into myself—the amalgam was never complete in my mind."[11] While the lens of Nick's divesting eye moves relentlessly in on Daisy, the details of Gatsby's life are purposely left vague and the reasons are not hard to find.

The double standard which makes Gatsby available for a romantic investment that Daisy cannot support also contributes one final play in the struggle for power that is the subject of *The Great Gatsby*. While Gatsby pays tribute to Daisy's position as an insider and invests his romantic fantasies in the image of her advantage, Nick reverses the process and, by turning things inside-out, creates the position of outsider as the ultimate object of romance. Behind the figure of Jay Gatsby, with his house and cars and money, is the image of James Gatz, the poor boy with his nose forever pressed against the window of a house he cannot enter. But if one is going to romanticize the position of outsider, as Nick finally does, surely Daisy, the excluded middle in Nick's romantic syllogism and thus the real outsider, is the logical choice. That its context makes this logic seem absurd defines the degree to which *The Great Gatsby* is based on the lie of a double standard that makes female characters in our "classic" literature not persons but symbols and makes women's experience no part of that literature's concern. But *The Great Gatsby* claims to be universal. What exempts Gatsby from the moral indictment which consumes the other characters in the book and what makes him a legitimate subject for romance are the symbolic dimensions of his vision and his self-creation. It is the purity of Gatsby's motives, the absence of the merely "personal" in his quest, that saves him. Gatsby is not interested in money and status for themselves but for the imaginative vantage points they offer, positions opposite a green light; and his real trade is not in bootleg liquor but in the "milk of wonder." His design for life is no individual scheme of self-aggrandizement but rather a symbolic structure linked to such imaginative ventures as the search for America and thus representative of the universal dreamings of all men.

Gatsby's universality is a constant theme in the critical commentary on the novel. Thus Marius Bewley: "Gatsby is not merely a likeable, romantic hero; he is a creature of myth in whom is incarnated the aspiration and the ordeal of his race." Thus Lionel Trilling: "Gatsby is said by some to be not quite credible, but the question of any literal credibility he may or may not have becomes trivial before the large significance he implies. For Gatsby, divided between power and dream, comes inevitably to stand for America itself." Thus William Troy: "It is this which makes the latter one of the few truly mythological creations in our recent literature—for what is mythology but this same process of projected wish fulfillment carried out on a larger scale and by the whole consciousness of a race?" Thus A. E. Dyson: "The squalor and splendor of Gatsby's dreams belong, I shall suggest, to the story of humanity itself; as also does the irony, and judgment, of his awakening."[12]

Surely any woman reading *The Great Gatsby* is justified in

discounting somewhat this much touted universality. For if, in the words of Bewley, "the true question is not what Gatsby sees in Daisy, but the direction he takes from her, what he sees *beyond* her," and if the "element of grandeur" in this vision beyond is the fact that "for Gatsby, Daisy does not exist in herself,"[13] then this universality, which is the highly acclaimed end justifying the means, is anything but universal and the imaginative structures to which the book gives such brilliant expression are merely those of all *men*. The structures of the romantic imagination, whether the object of investment be male or female, are affairs of the male ego from which women are excluded. Thus, the view of Daisy as an insider is as much a lie as the view of Gatsby as an outsider. To be contained immobile (the magical formulating phrase exists without benefit of verb) inside a white palace is to be effectively locked out, just as to be outside the palace looking up and creating the imaginative structures which define it is to be in control and hence, in any meaningful sense of the word, inside. For "high in a white palace" is precisely where the romantic imagination of Gatsby/Carraway/Fitzgerald wants to keep "the king's daughter, the golden girl," because finally that imagination wants women to be kept outside so that they can remain forever available as occasions for the heroic gestures of men and as scapegoats for the failure of men's dreams. The "impersonality" of Gatsby is a rather personal affair after all.

The exclusion of women from the meaning of universal is not new. However, the form this dishonesty takes in *The Great Gatsby* is particularly virulent because in reading the novel women are asked to accept someone as heroic precisely because they do not exist for him. While Gatsby pays for his imagination, Daisy pays more. In being seized as the incarnation of his dream, Daisy is annihilated as a separate person and is solipsized into Gatsby, becoming an extension of him. This is why Gatsby can react with such incredulity when Nick suggests that it may be asking a bit much of Daisy to insist that she repudiate her life with Tom and act as if it never happened. And this is why he responds with such disbelief when finally confronted with Daisy's child, living proof that she has had a life with Tom separate from him. Because for Gatsby, of course, Daisy does not exist apart from him and he cannot accept the fact of any experience of hers that does not fit in with his conception of her. This point is made in the scene following the accident in which Myrtle Wilson is killed. Nick returns to the Buchanans' house and finds Gatsby in his archetypal position, outside, "watching": "She's locked herself in her room, and if he tries any brutality she's going to turn the light out and on again" (p. 145). Daisy, however, is not palpitating in her room waiting for a brutal Tom to threaten her so that she may signal to her lover outside to rush in and save her. Rather, she is sitting in the pantry having a cold supper with her husband. But it is obvious that in order to get rid of Gatsby, Daisy has had to tell him a story out of *his* imagination. And what that imgination requires is that she remain a fantasy, locked up in a high, white palace, outside, unreal, and ultimately nonexistent. Thus, when Nick says that he left Gatsby that night "watching over nothing," the phrase moves beyond the need to devalue Daisy and reveal her essential emptiness and turns back upon Gatsby to imply that the nothing he is watching over is the empty room his own solipsism has constructed.

For certainly there is in the Carraway/Fitzgerald mind an element that is genuinely and meaningfully critical of the Gatsby imagination and that exposes rather than imitates it. The scene in which Tom and Gatsby confront each other to fight over Daisy involves a rather self-conscious exposure of the romantic pose of "protector of fair womanhood" which each of them tries to appropriate for himself. There is indeed some recognition of the fact that Daisy's choices amount in reality to no more than the choice of which form she wishes her oppression to take. And a critical perspective is behind the way Nick shapes his account of what Gatsby demands from Daisy: "He wanted nothing less of Daisy than that she should go to Tom and say: 'I never loved you'" (p. 111). The emphasis here, unlike that of most references to Daisy, is on "nothing less" rather than on "she." At some level there is a recognition of the fact that the weight that Gatsby's imagination brings to bear on Daisy is unbearable and that the failure of the dream is not in Daisy herself but is rather the inevitable result of the internal dynamics of the imagination which seizes her as the object of its dreaming. Thus, the significance of the "distortions" of West Egg which brood over Nick's memory and over the closing pages of *The Great Gatsby* goes beyond the registering of the full measure of Nick's animus, his need to divest Daisy of the magic of her voice and Jordan of the potency of her name, to record that foul dust which is in fact the product of the romantic imagination: "In the foreground four solemn men in dress suits are walking along the sidewalk with a stretcher on which lies a drunken woman in a white evening dress. Her hand, which dangles over the side, sparkles cold with jewels. Gravely the men turn in at a house— the wrong house. But no one knows the woman's name, and no one cares."

FOUR

THE BOSTONIANS
Henry James's Eternal Triangle

I

The Bostonians is of particular interest to the feminist critic because the critical commentary on it provides irrefutable documentation of the fact that literary criticism is a political act—that it derives from and depends on a set of values, usually unarticulated and unexamined, in the mind of the critic and that it functions to propagate those values. To demonstrate this point I have chosen to begin this chapter with extended "extracts" from the body of critical commentary and with a detailed analysis of it. I have tried to arrange the selections so as to define most sharply the values, the necessities, and the "logic" of that collective creature whose existence and whose purpose they reveal: the phallic critic.[1] There is no better context for my own reading of *The Bostonians* than that provided by these extracts.

The Critics

1. The subject is strong and good, with a large rich interest. The relation of the two girls should be a study of one of those friendships between women which are so common in New England. The whole thing as local, as American, as possible, and as full of Boston: an attempt to show that I *can* write an American story. . . . At any rate, the subject is very national, very typical. I wished to write a very *American* tale, a tale very characteristic of our social conditions, and I asked myself what was the most salient and peculiar point in our social life. The answer was: the situation of women, the decline of the sentiment of sex, the agitation in their behalf.

—*The Notebooks of Henry James,* ed. F.O. Matthiessen and Kenneth B. Murdock (New York: Oxford University Press, 1947), p. 47.

2. *The Bostonians* charts the parallel disarrangement, sometimes verging on a derangement, of public and private, political and sexual life. James was bold enough to see that the two spheres of experience could not be kept apart, and that it would be a fatal error for a novelist if he tried to. He was even bolder in supposing that the ideological obsessions which form so constant a peril for public life will leave their mark, not merely on social behavior, but also on the most intimate areas of private experience.

—Irving Howe, Introduction, *The Bostonians* (New York: Random, 1956), xiv.

3. If we compare the two political movements which James undertook to represent, the revolutionary anarchism of *The Princess Casamassima* will perhaps on first inspection seem to promise more as a theme for a novel than the militant feminism of *The Bostonians.* In a struggle for general social justice there is a natural force and dignity; and in a violent revolutionary intention there is the immediate possibility of high tragedy. But the doctrinaire demand for the equality of the sexes may well seem to promise but a wry and constricted story, a tale of mere eccentricity. . . . There is indeed some unpleasantness in the comedy

of *The Bostonians*, yet exactly by risking this, by daring to seize on the qualities of the women's-rights movement which were "unnatural" and morbid, James possessed himself of a subject which was even larger in its significance than that of *The Princess Casamassima*. A movement of social revolution may question the culture in which it exists, or it may not—indeed, we can say of social revolutions that they do not in fact question culture as much as they seem to do and say they do. But a movement of sexual revolution is to be understood as a question which a culture puts to itself, and right down to its very roots. It is a question about what it means to be a man and what it means to be a woman—about the quality of being which people wish to have.

And the fear of the loss of manhood . . . is given reason for its existence everywhere in *The Bostonians*. The book is full of malign, archaic influences; it is suffused with primitive fear. . . . Basil Ransom is explicit in his feeling that when he is with Olive Chancellor he is not "safe." And indeed his position is at all times a precarious one. . . . Perhaps the novel's crucial scene is that which takes place in Memorial Hall at Harvard, when Ransom finds it necessary to enforce upon Verena's imagination the pathos of the fate of the young men who had died in the recent war. These young men had been his enemies, but he feels bound to them by the ties of the sex they have in common, and the danger of battle had never been so great as the sexual danger of his present civil situation (pp. 114-15).

During his sad visit to his parental land in 1883, the last for twenty years, when the parental family had come to an end, Henry James wrote out the scenario of *The Bostonians*, which is a story of the parental house divided against itself, of the keystone falling from the arch, of the sacred mothers refusing their commission and the sacred fathers endangered (p. 117).

—Lionel Trilling, *The Opposing Self* (New York: Viking, 1955), pp. 109-110.

4. What Olive does not see is that the freedom she would win for women is pitched at an absolute level that strikes at the heterosexual basis of human existence. . . . Homosexuality in

Olive is the biological evidence of a rigid self-centeredness that has blinded itself to the heterogeneous character of reality.

—William McMurray, "Pragmatic Realism in *The Bostonians*," *19th Century Fiction*, 16 (March, 1962), 341.

5. But on Olive's part it is more than a friendship; she is pretty distinctly a case of perverse sexuality; and whether or not James knew what he was doing, he had certainly observed curiously some real instance of Olive's derangement.

—F.W. Dupee, *Henry James* (New York: Dell, 1965), p. 131.

6. The psychological motivation for Olive Chancellor's agitation on behalf of her own sex he astutely conceived as hatred or at least fear of the opposite sex—in a word, incipient Lesbianism—though he phrased it indirectly as "one of those friendships between women that are so common in New England." . . . As a foil to Boston's latter-day saints he knew he needed a young man "who, being of a hard-headed and conservative disposition, is resolutely opposed to female suffrage and all such alterations." Also, as the opposition to this unnatural friendship between the two young women he was to be the embodiment of the sentiment of sex, in love with the heroine Verena and determined to snatch her from the clutches of her reformer friend.

—Charles R. Anderson, "James's Portrait of the Southerner," *American Literature*, 27 (1955), 310.

7. Romance and James are on the side of Ransom. Without encumbering the story with Lesbianism, one can still recognize in Olive's obsession a serious evil. If Verena were not dramatically rescued by Ransom, she would be in danger of the loss of her very freedom itself.

—Walter F. Wright, *The Madness of Art: A Study of Henry James* (Lincoln: University of Nebraska Press, 1962), p. 95.

8. The tears Verena is to shed in the future are, after all, a small price to pay for achieving a normal relationship in a society so

sick. A spring and summer courtship cannot last forever, but the
marriage affirms nature's ability ever to renew itself.

   —Robert C. McLean, *"The Bostonians:* New England Pasto-
ral," *Papers on Language and Literature,* 7 (Fall, 1971), 381.

9. It is precisely here that James's depoliticizing has a harmful
consequence. For, no less than Olive, Basil is seeking to annex
Verena Tarrant because he loves her. I do not think that James
meant us to take their claims as equally meritorious, but the
question needn't have come up . . . (p. 102).

More serious than these equations between the combatants,
which after all might be attributed to evaluative sophistication, is
a stream of jokes at Basil's expense that is gratuitous, if not
downright silly . . . (p. 103).

Though James may blur the relative merits of his antagonists in
the manner I have outlined, on one issue he never sways: men
and women are unique in their gifts and privately precious to
each other for that reason. Even Miss Birdseye, a combination of
futile busybody and selfless reformer, is ultimately valuable because she has not, like the more recent Bostonians, lost sight of
her undeniable self; "Miss Birdseye, for all her absence of profile," Ransom eventually decides, remained "essentially
feminine" (p. 106).

   —Charles T. Samuels, *The Ambiguity of Henry James* (Urbana:
University of Illinois Press, 1971).

10. Admittedly Basil's conservative politics preserve his own
humanity just as revolutionary liberalism erodes Olive's personal
being. Specifically, Basil's conservatism allows him to keep his
capacity for sexual feeling. Indeed, his conservatism is his only
defense against psychological castration. . . . Unlike Olive, Basil,
the conservative, does not have his emotions inverted. . .(p. 340).

But the trouble is that the image of Basil as romantic conservative is not at all stable. . . . The gamut of images, as we shall see,
becomes at times almost schizophrenic . . . (p. 341).

Basil still remains preferable to Olive—the young Southerner retains his humanity—but that is his one advantage (p. 343).

—Theodore C. Miller, "The Muddled Politics of Henry James's *The Bostonians," Georgia Review,* 26 (1972).

11. Ransom wins. Despite all of James' qualifications in regard to Ransom, he grants him certain attractions and powers. . . . But the logic of the book itself demands that Ransom win. For if the struggle between Ransom and Olive over Verena is a struggle between competing ideologies over a passive agent of the natural and the human, then it is a struggle between ideologies that are not equally in opposition to the natural and the human. When she is finally driven to her choice, Verena chooses in accordance with those rhythms of life which Olive bluntly violates but Ransom merely exploits (Howe, xxvii-viii).

12. The reader is made to believe to some degree that in the struggle between Olive and Ransom he is watching a struggle between good and evil. . . . But again he offers a struggle in reality between mirror-images. Ransom and Olive are both profound egotists. Neither loves Verena for herself; she is something to be acquired and possessed and used as an instrument of a personal idea; Ransom is almost as much interested in defeating Olive as in marrying Verena. And Olive is too morbid and hysterical and jealous to make us believe she has Verena's good at heart. Here again those who have read the novel as "lesbian" tend to see Ransom in a better light than James represents him—for they read him in the belief that he is rescuing Verena from Olive's depravity. The truth is that James has little respect for either. It is their struggle for power which he finds fascinating: they are ruthless, self-seeking, blind to the feelings of others and aware only of their own needs.

—Leon Edel, *Henry James: The Middle Years* (Philadelphia: Lippincott, 1962), p. 141.

13. But are we then to assume that the love of Verena and Ransom is "really" personal in some sense?—heterosexual being better than lesbian, in spite of its grotesque variants in the book.

. . . Eventually it comes to the question of the nature of the relationship, the union. And uncertainties and forebodings about that do not spring from the novel's grim last sentence alone. . . . If this is the most substantial relationship in the book (although one would have to say that the Olive-Verena affair is the more subtle, also involving as it does a rationale of free union), it is because it takes up and confirms what all other "unions" point to. dominance for one partner, defeat for the other. That is the force of sexuality in the novel.

—David Howard, "The Bostonians," in *The Air of Reality: New Essays on Henry James,* ed. John Goode (London: Methuen, 1972), pp. 71-72.

14. Apropos of the satirical treatment of Feminism, one might mention an act of historical justice fortuitously performed many years later, when Sargent's famous portrait of James, on exhibition at the Royal Academy in London, was set upon and mutilated by a band of marauding suffragettes. These female militants were quite unaware of the satire on their cause composed by the distinguished gentleman shown in Sargent's portrait. As for the distinguished gentleman himself, no doubt he felt that they had selected exactly the right object on which to vent their fury.

—Philip Rahv, Introduction, *The Bostonians* (New York: Dial Press, 1945), ix.

II

When one surveys the critical commentary on *The Bostonians,* one is struck by its relentless sameness. While the criticism on *A Farewell to Arms* and *The Great Gatsby* shares major biases and blind spots, there is nevertheless a kind of ongoing debate within it. In the case of *A Farewell to Arms,* the debate has to do primarily with Hemingway's attitude toward and evaluation of the love affair between

Catherine and Frederic and with the question of Frederic Henry's character. In the case of *The Great Gatsby,* the debate is in part over the question of whether the book is a criticism of America for failing to provide its young men with adequate dreams or whether it is a criticism of the nature of the dream itself; and in part it is over the question of the role of the narrator. This debate, however, is a luxury made possible by the fact that neither novel forces the critic to raise certain questions. One can avoid in *A Farewell to Arms* the hostility toward Catherine and its implications for the nature of romantic love, because that hostility is so well disguised and because the disguise is so common in sexist society. For similar reasons one can ignore the double-standard in *The Great Gatsby* and the implications of the scapegoating of Daisy. But the subjects of women, of their relation to society and to each other, and of men's relation to them are unavoidable in any discussion of *The Bostonians,* because it is James's avowed intention to raise in his novel "the situation of women." The unavoidable subject of women provides the key to the critics' reading of *The Bostonians.* Lionel Trilling's description of the atmosphere of the novel can be applied with equal, if not greater, accuracy to the criticism of it, for that criticism is indeed "suffused with a primitive fear." Scenting danger in the implications of James's subject matter, the critics respond in the same manner Trilling accords to Ransom in that crucial scene in the Harvard yard: in the face of a common enemy they bury their impulse to fraternal war and band together under the aegis of the sex they share to defeat the one they aren't. A common "fear of the loss of manhood" may well overcome a multitude of differences that would under less threatening circumstances find expression.[2]

The Bostonians scares the phallic critic. It is hardly irrelevant that Philip Rahv ends his brief introduction to the Dial Press edition of the novel with a mocking reference to

the mutilation of James's portrait by the London suffragettes. The need to mock is as revealing as the need to refer.
The reasons for this fear should be clear from the comments of Howe, Trilling, and McMurray I've selected: *The
Bostonians* raises questions that strike at the root of "the
heterosexual basis of existence"; it raises the question
about "what it means to be a man and what it means to be a
woman." While Trilling is perhaps the most honest of the
critics in defining the exact nature of this fear, it is apparent that what male critics see in *The Bostonians* is an embat
tled phallic principle making a desperate stand against the
odds of James's particular version of the castrating bitch.[3]

The analysis of the phallic critic derives from this primal
reaction. In the remarks of McMurray we can see the first
stage of this analysis, from which all the other stages may
be easily enough deduced: "What Olive does not see is that
the freedom she would win for women is pitched at an
absolute level that strikes at the heterosexual basis of
human existence. . . . Homosexuality in Olive is the biological evidence of a rigid self-centeredness that has blinded
itself to the heterogeneous character of reality." Beginning
with the comforting assumption that Olive does not know
what she is about, McMurray instinctively moves from the
view of Olive as a serious threat to what *he* conceives as
absolute for human existence, namely heterosexuality, to
defining her as lesbian; he then treats homosexuality as
pathological and invokes it as proof that Olive's desires
and interests are in fact "rigid self-centeredness"; and this,
finally, he equates with blindness to the "heterogeneous
character of reality," which he in turn equates with heterosexuality, returning thus to his original starting point. The
unquestioned assumptions in this chain of "reasoning" are
so numerous as to stupefy. Yet, to a greater or lesser degree, such unexamined thinking obtains in all the criticism. For, as McMurray demonstrates, it is in the imputation of lesbianism, with all its assumed connotations, that

the phallic critic feels he has irrefutable evidence for his reading of the book. To associate Olive with lesbianism is, in the critics' eye, to define her as odious, perverse, abnormal, unnatural—in a word, evil. Even those critics who hesitate to apply the label do so in such a way as to intensify both its possibility and the horror inherent in it. From this view of Olive it is but a single, inevitable step (as the remarks of Anderson demonstrate) to the vision of Ransom as hero, the knight in shining armor, the repository of all that is healthy, sane, and good; and from here it is but another single step to the melodramatic reading of the novel as the rescue of Verena from perversion, exploitation, imprisonment, death—the snow-white maiden saved from the clutches of the wicked witch by the handsome prince.

There are, of course, among the critics those who resist the easy strategy of melodrama because they perceive what would seem to be obvious to anyone reading the book— that is, James's considerable ambivalence toward the figure of Ransom and the parallels which exist between him and Olive. While the responses of these critics to this perception differ, there are crucial similarities. First, the support for their final positions resides inevitably in an appeal to values which exist (or, better, are assumed to exist) outside the framework of the novel. The views expressed rely on external support to such an extent, in fact, that evidence from within the novel is assumed to be unnecessary or, if invoked at all, is handled in a thoroughly arbitrary manner. Thus Samuels offers as proof for his final position that "on one issue [James] never sways," the evidence that Miss Birdseye "is ultimately valuable because she has not, like the more recent Bostonians, lost sight of her undeniable self." And his support for this assessment of Miss Birdseye lies in the assertion that, in Ransom's eyes, Miss Birdseye remains "for all her absence of profile . . . essentially feminine." Second, each critic adopts the same format for discussing the novel. Each begins with an attack upon Olive. This attack is followed by a discussion of Ransom, couched in positive terms. Even in those instances when the critic wishes to get right to the point of Ransom's limitations, the language used on him is so different in emotional tone and moral value from that used on Olive that one is amazed to discover at the end that the remarks are intended as criticism. Then there ensues some version of the fairy-tale reading of the story. Only after all this "introduction" has taken place does the writer suggest that there may be some serious problems with Ransom's character. This format lessens the impact of the criticism of Ransom and leaves the fairy-tale version of the story essentially intact. The resultant analysis is understandably muddled.

Samuels and Miller are representative of those critics who see the complexity surrounding Ransom's character as a lamentable lapse on James's part and a failure of aesthetic control. Here the need to hang on to the phallic interpretation of the novel, despite all evidence to the contrary, is seen in its crudest form. Howe is representative of those critics who, while they clearly see and freely admit the similarities in character and behavior between Olive and Ransom, nevertheless insist on evaluating them quite differently. Thus, what is pathological in Olive is, at most, a limitation in Ransom. In Howe's analysis, Ransom wins, despite all that is problematical about him, because he is finally on the side of nature. When Verena chooses, she "chooses in accordance with those rhythms of life which Olive bluntly violates but Ransom merely exploits." While Howe attributes Ransom's triumph to the logic of the book, the logic invoked is finally his own and it is, when the elegant rhetoric and the elegiac tone are cleared away, much the same "logic" as that which produces the fatuousness of writers like Samuels and McClean. For the "argument from nature," despite all pretensions to the contrary, is simply the biggest phallic gun of them all, used to support an interpretation which is not so much what James wrote as what the critic wants.

There is only one critic who seems capable of questioning the values which implicitly govern the phallic critic's analysis, and that is David Howard. Howard is willing to raise the question of whether or not James is on the side of heterosexuality in *The Bostonians* and of whether or not, if the book is in fact a triumph of the forces of "nature," James does not view these forces as odious and in themselves perverse. (It is perhaps not irrelevant that Howard is English.) Even Edel, in his spirited denunciation of the melodramatic reading of the book, does not question the values upon which such a reading rests. He would remove lesbianism from the reading of the novel precisely because it is such a powerful incentive for what he sees as a misinterpretation, not because he thinks James might have a different attitude toward it than the common response.

The lone voice of Howard, nevertheless, poses the question of how much the phallic critic's reading of *The Bostonians* is actually in the book and how much of it is in the psychological needs of his own fantasy life. A critic like Anderson has a vision of what *The Bostonians* ought to be about, and his criticism of James takes the form of berating him for not having written the novel which he, Anderson, has in mind: "The author should have confined his treatment of Southern conservatism to suggesting that the stability of Southern society was due to its emphasis on family, and that it provided a clearly defined civilization in which his hero could operate as a man of principle."[4] It is but a short step from this kind of projection to the subtle rewriting we get from critics like Dupee and Samuels: "But on Olive's part it is more than a friendship; she is pretty distinctly a case of perverse sexuality"; "As the lovers make their frantic exit, James denies that Verena will live happily ever after, but she will live." Indeed, if the criticism of

The Bostonians is remarkable for its relentless sameness, its reliance on values outside the novel, and its cavalier dismissal of the need for textual support, it is equally remarkable for its failure to invoke any evidence from James himself. If, for a moment, we look at what James in fact says about *The Bostonians*, we may perhaps see why this is so:

> The subject is strong and good, with a large rich interest. The relation of the two girls should be a study of one of those friendships between women which are so common in New England. The whole thing as local, as American, as possible, and as full of Boston: an attempt to show that I *can* write an American story. . . . I asked myself what was the most salient and peculiar point in our social life. The answer was: the situation of women, the decline of the sentiment of sex, the agitation in their behalf.

What is most striking about James's comments in his notebooks is their lack of congruence with the value system of the phallic critic. At no point does James even faintly suggest that he is writing a novel about the abnormal, the unnatural, the perverse, or that the drama of the story resides in pitting the forces of health and sanity against those of depravity. While he lays out the scenario for *The Bostonians* in considerable detail, his interest is not in such melodramatic possibilities but in the Americanness of the story and in the way in which it will prove that he can, in fact, do the local scene. One would be hard pressed to extract from James's presentation any relative evaluation of his characters or any moral stance toward his plot. And when he describes the most salient feature of the local scene, his language is remarkably neutral: "the situation of women, the decline of the sentiment of sex, the agitation in their behalf." While these phrases have been used to support a theory of James's antifeminism, it is hard to see how. Only the second has a hint of value judgment in it, and beyond the fact of its rather strange placement between the other two—a position which certainly weakens its impact as any statement of attitude—it is finally impossible to know what James means by "the sentiment of sex"; and if we do not know what James means by it, we can hardly know what he felt about it.

Nor is there anything in James's language describing the relation between Olive and Verena to justify the interpretation the phallic critic gives it. James defines the relation between Olive and Verena as a friendship which, far from being unnatural, is a *common* feature of the New England experience. Much is made of the impact on the writing of *The Bostonians* of James's visits to America in 1881-82 and 1882-83, and of the death of his mother and the subsequent death of his father. Yet, not one critic whom I have read, with the exception of Leon Edel, has mentioned what would seem to be an obvious familial influence and one of potentially far more importance to *The Bostonians* than the parental deaths—namely, Henry's sister, Alice James, who was herself involved in one of those friendships which the brother saw as so common to New England soil. During the period of his second stay in America in 1883, Henry and Alice lived together and James wrote to his London publisher that "my sister and I make an harmonious little *ménage,* and I feel a good deal as if I were married."[5] Edel describes the experience as follows: "The bachelor son and the spinster daughter seem to have found much peace and harmony in being together. . . . They had always felt an intimate kinship that transcended ties of family, a strong emotional compatibility reaching back to their early years. . . . He felt for her a peculiar and intense affection, such as he was to describe in some notes for a story he never wrote. . . ."[6]

During this time James had ample opportunity to observe Alice's friend, Katherine Loring, and "to recognize," as Edel puts it, "the beginning for his sister of a close and, as it proved, an abiding attachment."[7] Shortly after James's return to England in the summer of 1883, Alice and Katherine followed, and from then until the end of her life, Alice was in close contact with Henry. James's notebook entry for *The Bostonians* is dated April 8, 1883— that is, during the period when he was living with Alice— and his writing of the novel largely coincides with the first few months of Alice's settling in England. Thus, if one can ignore for the moment the arrogant bias of Dupee's comment, it would appear to be the case that James "had certainly observed curiously some real instance of Olive's derangement." Yet derangement seems no part of James's vision of Alice's relationship with Katherine Loring, whom he described as characterized by "a devotion so perfect and so generous" as to be "a gift of providence."[8] Indeed, James's understanding of their relationship, though at times critical, is imbued by a genuine sympathy. Thus, if one looks to the external context surrounding the conception of *The Bostonians*, one can find only support for the love between Olive and Verena. That this context is consistently ignored in critical discussion of *The Bostonians* is simply one more proof of the subjectivity of that criticism and of its inherently political nature. For if one approaches *The Bostonians* with a different subjectivity, one that does not have at its heart the "despairing cry: *It is too late, there is no place for the sensitive and thoughtful man, perhaps there never was,*"[9] but rather is inspired by a sense of the tragic fate which awaits the sensitive and thoughtful woman in a patriarchal culture, one will find in James's novel a drama and a meaning quite other than that embodied in the critics' assessments.

III

When James chose "the situation of women" as the quintessential subject for his very American tale, he was countering a bias as central to American literature as the point he was making is central to American culture. As the other chapters of this book have demonstrated, American literature is a masculine territory in which the situation of women, if dealt with at all, is dealt with indirectly and primarily in terms of its effects on men. While no one would want to make a claim for James as an ardent or perhaps any other kind of feminist, still he has the ability to place himself on the side of women and in line with their point of view. *The Bostonians* is a case in point. Although James takes the material necessary to flesh out his subject and his plot from his sense of the women's rights movement in the Boston of the 1870s, nevertheless the satire and irony that play about this "flesh" have less to do with James's feelings about feminism than with his feelings about reform and reformers. In fact, the real subject of the novel is deeply feminist, engaging James's considerable interest and producing some of his sharpest perceptions. As Irving Howe points out, James was quite aware of the connection between the personal and the political, but James's daring lies not, as Howe claims, in his moving from the public to the private but rather in his moving from the private to the public. That is, the perception at the heart of *The Bostonians* is not that "ideological obsessions . . . will leave their mark . . . on the most intimate areas of private experience," but rather that the conditions of one's private life will determine the nature of one's ideology. When the subject is women, this reversal is particularly crucial, since women are by definition private property and by experience private creatures. Thus, if one wishes to treat women accurately and seriously, one must grant primacy to the private sphere. While Howe seeks to undermine the valid-

ity of Olive's private experience by seeing it as the scar of
an ideological obsession, James does precisely the opposite, for he grounds his story in an intensely personal
struggle and sees in it the defining condition of his country
and his culture.

In its vision of the relation between private and public,
personal and political, *The Bostonians* is a book about
feminism. It is also a book about feminism in that its actual
subject—power and powerlessness—is overtly sex-linked.
This is the burden of the particular version of the "eternal
triangle" which James has chosen to construct for his fable:
a man and woman struggle for the love and possession of
another woman, and the man wins, and the question is
why. And it is also in part the burden of James's invocation
of the Civil War as a background for the drama of his
story. In choosing to see "the situation of women, the decline of the sentiment of sex," as the crucial American subject rather than the Civil War, in choosing to write about
the Bostonians rather than about the great national
conflict, James suggests that a war in which men fight each
other is of less cultural importance than the struggle between men and women and of less significance than the
civil war within women. Thus, while *The Bostonians* is pervaded by a contempt for the nature and efficacy of movements and by a settled pessimism about the fate of women,
it nevertheless presents a striking analysis of the conditions
that feminism speaks to and of the problems that feminist
solutions must handle.

A final introductory point concerns James's attitude
toward Olive. Though it is true that James gives no explicit
endorsement of either the feminist or the antifeminist
view and that he treats both feminism and male
chauvinism with an equal degree of seriousness and an
equal degree of irony, still there is a sense in which James's
sympathies are not so evenly balanced as his irony would
make it appear. It would seem that James's discomfort

with the more aggressive aspects of male sexuality has its analogue in a sensitivity to those who are without the kind of power which that sexuality symbolizes. Surely part of James's pervasive affinity with women stems from his perception of them as underdogs. Unlike Fitzgerald, James is able to see that the real outsiders in American culture are women. Although this perception leads finally to a traditional response—that is, it leads James to romanticize women precisely because of the qualitites they gain as a result of being outsiders—nevertheless, the sympathy is real and should inform our sense of James's treatment of Olive. Though F.O. Matthiessen is the sole exception to the universal critical attack on Olive, he has defined the central fact about James's relation to her: "In considering the new movement for women's rights, his interest was entirely in its effect upon a character like Olive Chancellor, who, as the most complex nature in his book and the one most typical of New England, enlisted the greatest share of his attention. He does not satirize her, he sees her as essentially tragic, although her possessiveness over Verena cannot help making her unattractive."[10] With James, the question of value is synonymous with the question of interest. Indeed, James "places" Ransom for us early and clearly when he notes that Olive's morbidity does not elicit Ransom's interest. The phallic critic is never more perversely blind than when he assumes that James identifies with a character who does not share his interests. While it is unlikely that James identifies very much with either Ransom or Olive, it is Olive who interests him: it is she who claims his attention, and it is she who achieves stature. For better or worse, *The Bostonians* is finally Olive Chancellor's book.

The struggle for power, implicit in *A Farewell to Arms* and *The Great Gatsby*, is at the very heart of *The Bostonians*. It is inherent in James's choice of locale for his pro-

tagonists, a confrontation between a Southerner and a
Bostonian obviously invoking a long history of enmity.
Yet, crucially, James subordinates this regional conflict to
the larger sexual one; in his eyes the battle between men
and women is the central national issue. That the two are
interrelated or, perhaps more accurately, that the sexual
conflict lies behind the regional, is suggested throughout
the book. The Bostonians are women, and Boston is representative of that element of reform which had so much to
do with bringing the forces behind the Civil War to a head.
This implicit connection is made explicit in a character like
Miss Birdseye, whose abolitionist activities are the subject
of national fame. Thus, it is easy for Ransom to locate the
source of the war in the misdirected and aggressive energy
of women and to attribute to a female force the responsibility for all his present difficulties. Ransom's struggle with
Olive is an outgrowth of his analysis of the national cata-
clysm and an effort to reverse it. If the Civil War was a
battle of the sexes in which men lost, then he will reconsti-
tute the struggle on different grounds, grounds where
men can win, and he will take revenge in the process.
Ransom's politics are as sexual as his sexuality is political.

While Ransom views his struggle with Olive as phallic
melodrama, James goes to considerable lengths to establish the political and economic bases for his views on the
proper relations of men and women. Disadvantaged,
struggling for economic survival, and denied that political
career which he feels he was by nature and right destined
to have and for which he still secretly yearns ("he had
always had a desire for public life; to cause one's ideas to
be embodied in national conduct appeared to him the
highest form of human enjoyment," *The Bostonians* [N.Y.:
Random, 1956], p. 193), he does not intend to let women
invade further what he sees as male territory. Women
constitute an economic and political threat to Ransom.
When he turns from the law to try to make a living by his

"opinions," he discovers that women are his rather formidable competitors; the fact that their style has preempted national taste makes it difficult for him to get a hearing for his own pieces ("he [Matthew Pardon] remarked, however, that a correspondent suffered a good deal today from the competition of the 'lady writers'; the sort of article they produced was sometimes more acceptable to the papers" [pp. 126-27]). Women dominate the lecture circuit and make a lucrative business of it. It is hardly irrelevant that what Ransom notices when he visits the Tarrant home in Cambridge is a biography of Mrs. Ada T.P. Foat, "the celebrated trance-lecturer," or that it is this book which produces in him such a contempt for the atmosphere in which Verena has been brought up and from which he intends to "save" her. Ransom's desire to save Verena, like his desire to keep her private, has an economic context. This context is essential for evaluating the disparity between the utter seriousness with which Ransom treats the possibilities of his own career as a public figure and the ridicule which he heaps upon the idea of such a life for Verena. While it is his "ambition to transmit from time to time to his female relations" twenty-dollar greenbacks, he would be the first to prevent, if he could, their having the opportunity to earn them for themselves (p. 194). Money is power, as Ransom indirectly recognizes when he dismisses as "base" and "unmanly" the fleeting temptation to marry Mrs. Luna for her money.

Galled by the sight of women enjoying what he does not have—thus Olive's relative economic independence forces from him the remark that "this cushioned feminine nest made him feel unhoused and underfed" (p. 17)—Ransom is clearly jealous and competitive in his relation to Verena. She is, after all, destined for the very career and success he craves for himself. His obsessive desire to interpose between her and the realization of this career is certainly motivated by jealousy. Yet, what could be more to his economic advantage than to strike such a blow against the woman's voice? Since Ransom is certain that the ideas to which Verena is giving currency have created a climate of opinion in which it is impossible for him to get published, stifling Verena can only enhance his own possibilities for being recognized. The acceptance of his article for publication is thus the turning point in Ransom's courtship of Verena: it is symbolic of his having regained control over what he sees as legitimately male territory; and it is therefore symbolic of his inevitable dominion over her and her inevitable capitulation to him.

Ransom wants women to be private rather than public because such an arrangement is economically advantageous; it reduces his competition and enhances his chance of success. But such an arrangement has an additional economic function for him. When women are private, their role is to provide emotional support for men in their struggles to succeed in the world. Ransom parries Verena's concern over the fate of her talent should she marry him by exclaiming, "Charming to me, charming to all the world? What will become of your charm?—is that what you want to know? It will be about five thousand times greater than it is now; that's what will become of it. We shall find plenty of room for your facility; it will lubricate our whole existence. . . . You won't sing in the Music Hall, but you will sing to me; you will sing to every one who knows you and approaches you" (p. 402). The vision of a male culture that lives parasitically on the appropriation of female energy is central to *The Bostonians*. Ransom wants Verena's talent for himself and with good reason. While Ransom never asks Verena a question about herself, is never concerned to know how she feels or thinks about anything, in fact shows no interest whatsoever in her as a person separate from his vision of her destiny and his need to have her submit to this vision, she is forever drawing him out, asking him about himself and his thoughts, and, at the very moment when he is most contemptuous of her, encouraging him in his effort to get published and hoping he will succeed. Indeed, it is because of her encouragement that he makes his final and successful assault on the publishing world.

Ransom dislikes the idea of women having power in personal relationships as much as he dislikes the idea of their having economic or political power; the two are, of course, related. He is consistently contemptuous of and annoyed by women's attempts to supererogate power in personal relationships, and the image of a male's becoming satellite in a female system is anathema to him. Thus, his condescending response to the "little variety-actress" who "had lately married, to his great amusement, and her husband had taken her on a wedding tour, which was to be at the same time professional" (p. 195). He is angered by the few attempts Verena makes to exert some control over their relationship: "he didn't like being dismissed, and was thinking of pretexts to linger"; "he had known that their expedition must end in a separation which could not be sweet, but he had counted on making some of the terms of it himself"; "I was furious that morning, when I learned your flight" (pp. 251, 349, 459).

Ransom does not enjoy being put in the position that he so cavalierly assigns to women. Indeed, his rage at Mrs. Luna's attempts to coerce his attendance on her by invoking his chivalry shows how little he is willing to have his own behavior determined by sex-role conventions. Anxious to press upon women the eternal obligation of being "delicate, agreeable creatures, whom Providence had placed under the protection of the bearded sex" (p. 197), he cannot abide the thought of being under obligation to a woman and he drops the tutelage of Mrs. Luna's son when it becomes apparent that this is happening. Obviously, Mrs. Luna's pursuit of Ransom has several analogies to his pursuit of Verena. Yet, while Ransom is happy to pursue, he cannot bear being pursued; passionate to possess, he is appalled at Mrs. Luna's assumption of him as her possession; delighted to patronize, he is disgusted at being matronized: "She delighted in the delapidated gentry . . . the fallen aristocracy . . . the despoiled patriciate, I say, whose attitude was noble and touching, and toward whom one might exercise a charity as discreet as their pride was sensitive" (p. 212).

Ransom is interested in power for himself, and he sees his contest with Olive for Verena as a struggle for power. It is obvious from the outset that in this contest Ransom is going to win, for he has unmistakably the psychology and the bearing of a victor. His conviction that, despite those disadvantages under which he may labor as a result of the accidents of fortune, the world has a place for him, his ease with himself, and his sense of being at home in the world—in a word, his power—is made clear in the opening scene of the book when he and Olive first encounter each other. Left alone for a few minutes in the drawing room, Ransom immediately possesses himself of the environment: "The gentleman had not even needed to sit down to become interested; apparently he had taken up the volume from a table as soon as he came in, and, standing there, after a single glance round the apartment, had lost himself in its pages" (pp. 3-4). What is significant about this passage is both the rapidity with which Ransom takes in the apartment and the ease with which he avails himself of its furnishings. There is no sense of impediment between his desiring something and his taking it. It is Olive, rather, who appears awkward, foreign, and ill at ease in her own home. Toward the end of the novel, when its full import is clearer, this scene is recapitulated. Olive again discovers Ransom in possession of her home, this time the house on Cape Cod; and when he reaches out and takes from Olive's hand the letters she has for Miss Birdseye, he once again succeeds in invading and taking over her world.

From start to finish Ransom has the bearing and behavior of one with power. While Ransom's Southernness is
often invoked by the critics to support their vision of his
disadvantage, it would seem more accurate to read it as
James's way of clarifying the extent of the power that Ransom derives from the fact of his sex. By making Ransom a
Southerner James establishes a connection between
maleness and power; whatever political and personal disadvantage Ransom suffers as a result of coming from the
conquered half of the nation is countered and outweighed
by the immense advantage that accrues to him as a result
of being male. In the world of *The Bostonians* sex is a larger
political category than region. This point is made clearly
and poignantly in the scene the critics so frequently cite as
central: Basil and Verena's visit to Harvard. Most critics
see the scene as a reflection of Ransom's innate generosity
of spirit, his possession of the "masculine character, the
ability to dare and endure, to know and yet not fear reality" (p. 343), or, as Trilling would have it, as evidence of
the instinctive bonding together of men in the face of the
common danger of aggressive womanhood. Yet, it is
possible to read the scene in quite a different way, to see in
it a statement of the reality rather than the mythology of
power and powerlessness, and to derive from it a quite
different view of Ransom's character.

Contemplating the Harvard Library, Ransom, "as he
took possession, in a comprehensive glance, of the wealth
and wisdom of the place," feels "more than ever the sore-
ness of an opportunity missed; but he abstained from expressing it (it was too deep for that) . . ." (p. 246). That
Ransom can view Harvard as an opportunity, whether
missed or achieved, is what matters. The language of this
passage curiously echoes that of the opening scene, and,
like that scene, it indicates Ransom's possession of a large
conviction that the world is by right his domain. He can
look at Harvard and say to his "charming guide": "This is

the place where I ought to have been . . . I should have had a good time if I had been able to study here" (p. 245). The irony in this scene derives from the position of his "charming guide." For Verena a Harvard education is hardly an opportunity missed; it was never an opportunity in the first place. Indeed, Verena's place in the world of Harvard is revealed shortly after Ransom's lament; "in a moment Verena had introduced him to a young lady, a friend of hers, who, as she explained, was working on the catalogue" (p. 246). The role of women in Harvard is, as Ransom wishes it to be everywhere, that of supportive satellite, doing the menial tasks which make male intellectual life possible. Thus, Ransom's perception of exclusion and loss takes on a different character in light of the dimension of Verena's exclusion from the same scene. And this ironic statement of the realities of power and powerlessness is underlined by the fact that Verena is the guide, the insider, supposedly showing her world to a foreigner.

Ransom's inclusion as male in spite of being a defeated Southerner and Verena's exclusion as female in spite of belonging to the victorious North is emphasized by their visit to Memorial Hall. Ransom can relate to Memorial Hall because the experience it symbolizes is something he has shared with the men of Harvard. It enshrines and memorializes him as much as it does his fallen "enemy." Verena has no real relation to this monument because she is completely excluded from the experience it represents and hence from the possibilities for self-realization it provides. She is therefore free to have a rather different attitude toward it than that of Ransom's sentimental reverie: "It's a real sin to put up such a building, just to glorify a lot of bloodshed. If it wasn't so majestic, I would have it pulled down" (p. 248). Ransom replies, with his usual heavy-handed irony, that this is an example of "delightful feminine logic," by which he means, of course, irrationality. But Verena's remark is quite logical from the point of view of one who has had nothing to do with the fighting of the war or the building of the memorial to it; and it exposes the illogic of Ransom's view that women "are at the bottom of all the wars" (p. 92). Verena in her own way perceives that war and its romanticization are male experiences in which she has no part save as a figure in the fantasy life of the men who pretend that they fight for women and then blame war on them.

The conviction of the absolute primacy of the male point of view—male values, male experience, male culture—creates in Ransom's head a psychological equivalent of the massive structure of Memorial Hall. Ransom wins because he knows he will and he knows he will because that is the way things are and the way things are is right. This is the reality behind the critics' assertion that nature is on the side of Ransom. The force on Ransom's side is not nature; it is tradition and the power that derives from being able to invoke as one's support "the way things are." Ransom's assumption that civilization is equivalent to the rights and interests of *men* is made clear in his attitude toward the temperance question: "for the idea of a meddling legislation on this subject filled him with rage; the taste of liquor being good to him, and his conviction strong that civilization itself would be in danger if it should fall into the power of a herd of vociferating women" (p. 50). His conviction that women are the legitimate possessions of men is voiced when he first sees Verena:

> He grew more impatient at last, not of the delay of the edifying voice . . . but of Tarrant's grotesque manipulations, which he resented as much as if he himself had felt their touch, and which seemed a dishonor to the passive maiden. They made him nervous, they made him angry, and it was only afterwards that he asked himself wherein they concerned him, and whether even a carpetbagger hadn't a right to do what he pleased with his daughter.
>
> (p. 60)

His belief that he is the kind of man women really want and that his view of their destiny reflects their own deepest yearning, whether they know it or not, is conveyed in his response to Verena's admiration of Henry Burrage for his interest in her movement: "And don't you despise him for it?" (p. 278).

The power that accrues from such massive egotism, such unimpeded self-assurance, such absolute conviction that one's rights are primary is, of course, immense. It simply never occurs to Ransom to question himself or to think that he may be wrong. Nor does it ever occur to him to give any weight to the feelings or needs of others. The self-centeredness implicit in the scene at Harvard becomes quite explicit by the end of the novel, when Ransom can openly declare his intent to "spoil" Olive and Verena's Cape Cod retreat and then, a few moments later, can plead with Verena not to "spoil" his "poor little holiday" (pp. 373, 378). Ransom gives no credence to Verena's efforts to escape him, no validity to that sense of self which pulls her away from him. While Olive can, and must, raise the specter of the possibility that her relation to Verena has been built upon illusion, it is no part of Ransom's character to question whether or not his vision of Verena is as much his fantasy as it is her desire. Ransom's imagination is built upon the useful simplicities of melodrama. His facility is for projecting difficulties outward—onto the accidents of fortune, the machinations of Olive, the forces trying to pervert and ruin Verena: "She was a touching, ingenuous victim, unconscious of the pernicious forces which were hurrying her to her ruin. With this idea of ruin there had already associated itself in the young man's mind, the idea—a good deal more dim and incomplete—of rescue" (pp. 253-54). The connection between the theory of a victim and the justification for playing the role of ransomer is clearly put. And so is the power that derives from the ability to simplify matters thus. But as the ironic undercurrents of the passage suggest, this fairy-tale formula, of which the critics are so enamored, is Ransom's; it is not James's.

Indeed, James's irony plays to a considerable extent over Ransom's self-serving simplifications. Major among them is Ransom's relation to his code of chivalry. There are numerous references in the novel to Ransom's chivalry, and his sense of himself as chivalrous contributes much to his self-esteem. Yet, James demonstrates that Ransom's code of chivalry is consistently accommodated to his self-interest. During Ransom's second visit to Boston, when he is trying to find a way to get Verena's address in Cambridge, he reflects at considerable length on the discourtesy of asking Olive for it. Nevertheless, he finds himself at her door, which "oddly enough, he was obliged to pass on his way to the mysterious suburb" (p. 217). At this moment Miss Birdseye issues forth and, chivalrically prompt, Ransom insists on accompanying her home, though this good woman has "trudged about the streets of Boston for fifty years" alone (p. 218). Ransom willingly uses the pretense of chivalry—"Doesn't it look as if you had my sympathy, when I get into a car on purpose to see you home"—to accomplish his real aim: "what he had got into the car with her for was precisely to make her talk" and, in the process of talking, to reveal Verena's address (pp. 219, 221). His deception of Miss Birdseye is compounded when he gets her to agree to remain silent about his visit. Thus, he drives a wedge between Olive and Miss Birdseye, as he will a few hours later between Olive and Verena, beginning a process which will culminate in Olive's terrible isolation at the end. Miss Birdseye's "Well, you *are* considerate" is almost as ironic as Ransom's final words to her: "You are not mistaken if you think I desire above all things that your weakness, your generosity, should be protected" (pp. 226, 412). We have seen how Ransom protects her weakness and her generosity: he works them for all they are worth, and they are worth a good deal.

It is in the scene at the Burrages', however, that James most fully exposes Ransom's chivalry, for in it he reveals chivalry to be a mask for self-interest. Earlier, Mrs. Luna has found Ransom's chivalry to be "unsatisfactory" because "it committed him to nothing in particular" (p. 203). Here she is given painful proof of the validity of her perception. When she puts Ransom's chivalry to the test by creating a situation in which, in order to be gallant, he would have to give up something he wants, she discovers that he feels no compunction in finally abandoning her. His "system . . . hadn't forseen such a case as this," for chivalry was never meant to be contrary to self-interest. Olive puts her finger on this fact just moments before Ransom's encounter with Mrs. Luna: "You mean that you have traced a certain line for them [his mother and his sisters] and that that's all you know about it! . . . You hold us in chains, and then, when we writhe in our agony, you say we don't behave prettily!" (pp. 258-59).

Ransom's ability to accommodate his definition of chivalry to his sense of his own self-interest is again clear late in the novel when he questions how much consideration he owes to Olive in the contest for Verena:

> He was not slow to decide that he owed her none. Chivalry had to do with one's relations with people one hated, not with those one loved. He didn't hate poor Miss Olive, though she might make him yet; and even if he did, any chivalry was all moonshine which should require him to give up the girl he adored in order that this third cousin should see he could be gallant. Chivalry was forbearance and generosity with regard to the weak; and there was nothing weak about Miss Olive, she was a fighting woman, and she would fight him to the death, giving him not an inch of odds.   (pp. 403-404)

The speciousness of Ransom's conclusion that he owes Olive nothing is evident from the incoherence of his reasoning. It is hard to see how chivalry can at once have to do

with "one's relations to people one hated" and be simulta-
neously "forbearance and generosity with regard to the
weak." But, more importantly, Ransom manages to ex-
clude Olive from both definitions; when chivalry has to do
with those one hates, Olive is "poor Miss Olive"; when it
has to do with the weak, she is "a fighting woman" who
"would fight him to the death." In both cases Olive is
exempt from real consideration. It is just this ability to
shift definitions and perceptions that gives Ransom his
power, for it allows him not merely to do what he wants
but to think well of himself while doing it. Olive's palpable
weakness elicits neither generosity nor forbearance from
Ransom, because it is not a weakness that admits to the
legitimacy of his strength. It presents no comforting, flat-
tering image of the self, and hence it can be dealt with as
ruthlessly as if it were power. As Olive says, a contest with
Mr. Ransom is not equal.

The final source of Ransom's power, the final brick in
the Memorial Hall in his head, is his attitude toward his
antagonists. In his contest with feminism Ransom has the
immense advantage of finding women contemptible, dis-
missable, laughable: "God forbid, madam! I consider
women have no business to be reasonable"; "that is delightful feminine logic"; "there you are—you women—all
over; always meaning yourselves, something personal, and
always thinking it is meant by others" (pp. 222, 248, 342).
Ransom's presumed elevation of women is as much an
admission of contempt as his outright diatribes. He likes
women well enough in their place, but the place to which
he consigns them indicates his opinion of them. It is no
accident that Ransom sees his conquered, broken South as
a "she"; such is the proper state for women—blighted,
wounded, wrapped in a cloak of silence, requiring his protection. If women take their line from him, admit their
weakness, throw themselves on his strength, and find their
fulfillment as a satellite in his system, then they are accept-

able. But let them challenge that system, and the response they trigger exposes the contempt behind the wish to elevate:

> From the most damnable feminization! I am so far from thinking, as you set forth the other night, that there is not enough woman in our general life, that it has long been pressed home to me that there is a great deal too much. The whole generation is womanized; the masculine tone is passing out of the world; it's a feminine, a nervous, hysterical, chattering, canting age, an age of hollow phrases and false delicacy and exaggerated solicitudes and coddled sensibilities, which, if we don't soon look out, will usher in the reign of mediocrity, of the feeblest and flattest and the most pretentious that has ever been. The masculine character, the ability to dare and endure, to know and yet not fear reality, to look the world in the face and take it for what it is—a very queer and partly very base mixture—that is what I want to preserve, or rather, as I may say, to recover; and I must tell you that I don't in the least care what becomes of you ladies while I make the attempt! (p. 343)

Ransom seems to view women as a sort of human disease, a deficiency in the species whose pernicious influence can be contained only by locking them up. With all admirable qualities categorically assigned to the masculine character and hence to men, and with the feminine equated with the damnable, it is difficult to understand why Ransom wishes to possess himself of any woman, especially one as feminine as Verena—a point which reminds us of the fact that the true subject of *The Bostonians* is not love but power.

IV

If Ransom has the psychology of the victor, Olive has the psychology of the loser; she is as destined for defeat as he is for triumph. Olive's "morbidity" is immediately apparent to Ransom, but while he is content to stop with the label, James insists that the interesting question is the cause. Although it is common to see Olive's morbidity as the result of her latent lesbianism, which in turn is the result of a pathological inability to relate to men, a rather different picture emerges if we start with Olive's "lesbianism," defined as a legitimate desire for a union, whether sexual or not, with another woman and for a life that is woman-centered and woman-defined. If we consider what her chances are for accomplishing this desire, we may see her morbidity not as the result of her lesbianism but as the result of her powerlessness to act it out, and her man-hating not as pathological or irrational but as an understandable reaction to the facts of her experience.

That powerlessness is the key to Olive's morbidity is palpable in *The Bostonians*. Trilling is correct when he describes the atmosphere of the novel as suffused by fear. The fear, however, is not Ransom's but Olive's. When Olive first meets Ransom it is she, not he, who is overwhelmed by the premonition of disaster. Olive's fear is apparent in everything she does. Fear clouds her intelligence, controls her life, and is her most pervasive and permanent emotion. She is afraid of being laughed at, she is afraid of not being just, she is afraid of speaking—"Olive had a fear of everything, but her greatest fear was of being afraid" (p. 14). Thus, she is willing to invoke disaster in order to prove to herself that she is not afraid. Clearly, fear is not only a reflection of the condition of powerlessness; it also creates the structures for the perpetuation of that condition.

In making Ransom a Southerner, James establishes a connection between maleness and power; in making Olive a Bostonian, he establishes a connection between being female and being powerless. Olive's position as a member of that part of the nation whose moral and economic interests have been legitimized and entrenched by victory provides her initially with some sources of power that are denied to Ransom. She is a member of a functioning society whose structures and traditions have not been interrupted by defeat; in this sense she has a place in the world which Ransom does not have. And she has money. These sources of power, in combination with her sex, give her an early advantage over Ransom in their contest for Verena. She has something to offer immediately; she can invite Verena to her home and eventually ask her to live there, using the attractiveness of her social position as lure and the force of her money to finalize the proposition. Yet, even as she engages in this apparently blatant exercise of power, Olive feels powerless. She must buy Verena's parents off from year to year, with always the possibility for a change of pocket if not of heart. Olive cannot secure her relationship with Verena, because there is no legal, moral, or psychological sanction for it. While Ransom presses upon Verena an offer for the outright and permanent purchase of her person on the basis of having one article accepted for publication, Olive, despite her wealth and her position, can make no equivalent offer. Nor can she counter Mrs. Burrage's offer to buy Verena for her son, Henry; rather she must bear Mrs. Burrage's taunting reference to her as Verena's "owner." The disparity between what is acceptable in men's relation to women and what is acceptable in women's relation to women is unmistakable.

Olive is the embattled figure in *The Bostonians*; she is fighting for her life and she is fighting alone. Ransom sees Olive's tragedy in the fact that "no one could help her," but more to the point is that no one really wants to (p. 12). Her social position, while apparently a source of power, is really useless because her society is willing to support the claims of everyone else—parents, suitors, newspaper correspondents, and particularly Ransom—to Verena, but not Olive's. Miss Birdseye is lost in a romantic fantasy about Verena's reconstruction of the handsome Southerner; Mrs. Burrage wants Verena for Henry; Mrs. Farrinder wants her for her wing of the movement; Dr. Prance is only too happy to assist Ransom; and Mrs. Luna is clearly no "sister." Olive is without support. That powerlessness should result from isolation and morbidity from both is not surprising. Olive is morbid because she is losing and she loses because she is morbid. It is the static quality of this equation that produces the images of rigidity associated with Olive. Though she actually moves about a good deal in the course of her drama, we think of her as remaining fixed in one place until, released at last by the dynamics of her self-destructiveness, she achieves all motion in one final rush upon her destiny.

Indeed, much of the force of James's analysis of power and powerlessness lies in his understanding of the connection between character and context. If Ransom wins because he knows he will because that is the way things are, Olive loses because she knows she will because that is the way things are. Olive cannot speak to Verena with the conviction of success so easy to Ransom because, finally, she does not herself believe in the legitimacy of their relationship. Her perception that the world will judge her "ferociously" should she keep Verena from forming other and potentially conflicting ties is internalized in her own sense of the sordidness of her transactions with Verena's parents and in her unwillingness to confront Verena with the fact of that transaction. Unsupported from without, Olive is undermined from within, and the analogue for Ransom's massive self-assurance is Olive's massive self-hatred. In contrast to Ransom's accommodating mind, which enables him both to get what he wants and to think well of himself in the process, Olive's mind is dominated by a ruthless conscience which operates as an enemy within, continually interposing between herself and her desires and continually presenting to her the data for self-condemnation. In his presentation of Olive as dominated by moral imperatives, James has captured a quintessential consequence of being female in a culture created by Ransoms. Olive's conscience is both an internalization of Ransom's endless imperatives as to what women should and should not be and an accurate reflection of the negative judgments that lie behind such imperatives. It would be ironic, were it not so predictable, that what Ransom hates most about Olive is her conscience and the fact that she takes life hard.

Olive's self-hatred, of which her conscience is the agent, is reflected throughout her character: in her shyness, her guilt, her penchant for renunciation—her favorite passage in *Faust* is the one on renunciation—even in her feminism. Unlike Ransom, who feels that circumstances have thwarted the realization of his potential, Olive spends her life trying to justify her existence because she does not believe in its value. She feels guilty for having money and cannot rest until she finds a use for it beyond herself. (One can't imagine Ransom feeling guilty for having wealth; on the contrary, he grinds his teeth at the sight of Olive's "nest" and contemplates with a sense of injury the "contrasts of the human lot.") Yet, Olive feels she has nothing to offer the movement but money. She is incapable of allowing herself pleasure except in the context of some higher good which justifies it. Only in this light can Verena's importance to Olive be fully grasped, for Verena offers Olive the possibility for pleasure which is justified and for justification which is pleasurable. Their work together in the movement legitimizes for Olive the personal pleasure of the relationship, just as Verena's relative poverty enables her to feel that in helping Verena she is being socially useful rather than merely self-indulgent. Indeed, Verena makes possible for Olive the realization of the sole vision of pleasure that she can allow herself: "while she

spoke the peaceful picture hung before her of still winter
evenings under the lamp, with falling snow outside, and
tea on a little table, and successful renderings, with a chosen companion, of Goethe" (p. 87). When Olive loses Verena, she loses everything; part of the cruelty of Ransom's
phallic melodrama is that, were he to lose, he could say no
such thing.

Perhaps the most significant sign of Olive's self-hatred,
and its concomitant self-destructiveness, is the focus of her
feminism. In contrast to Mrs. Farrinder, whose interest lies
in getting women's rights now, Olive's fascination lies in
the accumulated mass of the history of female suffering.
Yet, to focus on women's suffering rather than on their
suffrage is to focus on their powerlessness rather than on
their potential for acquiring power. Olive's vision of
women's history inspires not change but an endless repetition of humiliation and defeat. The rage that such a vision
engenders can result in no effective outward expression,
because it is baffled by the very image of male tyranny and
power which accompanies it. As a consequence, Olive's
rage turns in upon herself, making her the victim of her
own intensity. Even more disturbing is the fact that Olive
needs her vision of the condition of women to be true
because this vision at once defines and justifies her. Olive
has to suffer; that is her character and her condition.
Thus, if Ransom's sadism is elicited by her suffering,
Olive's masochism feeds on such elicitings. This dynamic
determines what happens in their initial encounter, in
which Olive's passionate intensity is engaged in invoking
the full dimensions of Ransom's opposition to her: " 'Are
you against our emanicipation?' she asked, turning a white
face on him in the momentary radiance of a street lamp.
. . . 'You hate it!' she exclaimed, in a low tone" (p. 25).

If Ransom and Olive are inverse images of each other in
terms of power, in more important ways they are mirror
images of each other. Olive's vision of the nature and fate

of women is finally the same as Ransom's. She presents no vision of "the way things are" that is different from his, because his assertions find an echoing chord in her own innermost beliefs. Olive believes ultimately neither in herself nor in women nor in their cause or movement. Her similarity to Ransom is not simply that they are both possessive, jealous, and conservative, but that they both see as inevitable the patriarchal system. And it is just here that the tragic consequences of that system are most sharply felt. Olive is finally as much her own enemy as Ransom is. She assists in his triumph and her defeat; and the weight of her powerlessness is added to the cumulative force of his power.

V

James provides an important commentary on Olive's character and situation through his handling of other female figures in the novel, one of whom is Olive's sister, Mrs. Luna. While critics are quick to imply that James's attitudes toward feminism can be deduced from the characters he associates with the movement, they never suggest that his attitude toward the traditional arrangement between men and women, perhaps what he means by the "sentiment of sex," can be inferred from Mrs. Luna. Yet, Mrs. Luna is surely archapostle, on the female side, of "the way things are," just as she is surely the most vapid and silly of the female figures in the book. While James may or may not have intended Mrs. Luna as a satiric comment on traditional femininity, he certainly did intend her as a comment on the nature and degree of power available to women who accept Ransom's system. Mrs. Luna incessantly proclaims her satisfaction at being a woman in a man's world and asserts her belief that the system of male prerogatives affords her as much power as she wants or needs. Her relationship to Ransom is, however, a study in powerlessness. Though she displays nothing but traditional feminine behavior, she is incapable of affecting his behavior or of getting what she wants. She cannot prevent his rejecting her in public and she can do nothing to equal that humiliation and injury. Despite Ransom's pronouncements about women's influence over men, his behavior indicates that men will be influenced only when they wish to be and will be set in motion only when they decide to move. Moreover, Mrs. Luna's attempts to exercise the kind of power that Ransom says his system affords those women who accept it result in making her obnoxious, trivial, and the object of his scorn. Her coy insinuations, her cute notes, and her "domestic" evenings are grotesque; but they are so because, like all feminine expressions of desire, they must perforce be indirect. In trying to get what she wants, Mrs. Luna loses, because the only channels open to her provide the conditions for denying her. Ransom's system really has room only for women who, like Verena, are essentially passive, have no will or desire of their own, and simply respond to the power of men.

Mrs. Tarrant is another version of the powerlessness that results from living a traditional female life. Dragged through the world by the will and whim of her husband (the question of her daily bread being subject to the vagaries of his waterproof), Mrs. Tarrant is an image of the degree to which the quality of a woman's existence is determined by the character and fate of her husband. Whatever slight social status she inherited from her abolitionist father is lost in her marriage to Selah, just as her hopes of rising socially through her daughter are lost through the latter's marriage to Ransom. The experience of the mother is rather frightening in its implications for the fate of the daughter, giving flesh to the future so grimly alluded to at the novel's end. And the implicit parallel between their destinies deepens the vision of women's powerlessness by obliterating individual differences through shared class. Despite Verena's considerable advantage of talent and beauty and charm, as a woman her fate will be the same as that of her most undistinguished mother, because they are both women. Mrs. Tarrant herself is not eager for Verena to meet this fate; and in urging upon her the advantages of an association with Olive, she seeks to spare her daughter, "for the implications of matrimony were for the most part wanting in brightness—consisted of a tired woman holding a baby over a furnace-register that emitted lukewarm air" (p. 100). Indeed, as the only overt comment in the book on woman's experience in marriage, it presents a striking contrast to the view Trilling sees as informing the writing of *The Bostonians*. He quotes from what he describes as James's "impassioned memorial" to his mother:

> It was the perfect mother's life—the life of a perfect wife. To bring her children into the world—to expend herself, for years, for their happiness and welfare—then, when they had reached a full maturity and were absorbed in the world and their own interests—to lay herself down in her ebbing strength and yield up her pure soul to the celestial power that had given her this divine commission.[11]

That there is nothing in *The Bostonians* even remotely resembling such a traditional image of fulfilled womanhood, if it does not raise questions about how seriously James himself embraced the view, should at the very least raise some doubts about whether his sympathies in this novel are disposed in favor of the traditional system.

But what about the power of the women in the novel who choose to lead nontraditional lives? There are two of them: Miss Birdseye and Dr. Prance. Although Miss Birdseye has spent her life in the heroic service of various social movements, it is hard to imagine her as a person of force, even in her prime. She is vague, bemused, and totally unaware of the realities of political power. Though Ransom protests a "deep aversion to the ineffectual," it is only ineffectuality in men that bothers him (p. 17). What endears Miss Birdseye to him is exactly that quality of ineffectuality that she so amply possesses. She is an image of the eccentric spinster, patronized and indulged and kept busy in the service of "humanity," which is, from the male point of view, a safe way to channel the unfortunate energies of women. (See Trilling's view of the difference between the thematic possibilities of *The Princess Casamassima* and *The Bostonians*.) Miss Birdseye presents no real threat to things as they are and provides no meaningful alternative to the traditional roles of women.

On the surface Dr. Prance seems very different from Miss Birdseye. Though her energies are similarly channeled into service, there is no imputation of ineffectuality about her. She is direct, she is purposeful, and she is completely professional. And her relationship to Miss Birdseye shows no trace of identification. Yet, their similarities are more substantial than their differences. If Ransom likes Miss Birdseye because she retains to the end her "essential femininity," which is to say her powerlessness, he likes Dr. Prance for the same reason: she is a male-identified woman who presents no more threat to his system than does the feminine Miss Birdseye. Because she has achieved what she wants as an individual, Dr. Prance is willing to believe that women as a class suffer no particular handicaps and face no especial discrimination. She continually refers the question of feminism to the context of a humanism which claims that men and women are the same and have the same desires and confront the same problems. In doing this, she ignores the evidence of her own life, the fact that she has only women patients, and the truth that the life she leads bears no resemblance to the life of any ordinary male doctor. Espousing humanism, she in fact takes on the added burdens of being a woman doctor and is prepared to remain in her basement forever. She insists on viewing the goals of feminism in light of a conservatism which declares that life at best is not worth much and that therefore the sacrifices involved in women's struggle to "have a better time" are pointless (p. 43). Dr. Prance has no interest in making her private revolution a public issue. She is content to live and die a breed unto herself, an isolated example without political implications. Obviously such a position is pleasing to Ransom; he sees her, quite rightly, as one of the boys and wishes he could offer her a cigar. What he doesn't do, significantly, is wonder, as he does with Olive, what sex Dr. Prance belongs to. Ransom's theory of perversion is as political as his theory of normalcy. Asexuality is normal and "lesbianism" is not, because the latter is threatening to him while the former is not. Indeed, the ultimate similarity between Miss Birdseye and Dr. Prance, as it is the ultimate indication of their mutual ineffectuality, is the degree to which each has given up her sexuality in order to accomplish her goals. Olive's potential effectuality can be measured by the fact that she is not so willing to do this.

It is Verena, however, who provides the most significant comment on the accuracy of Olive's perception of the powerlessness of women and on the legitimacy of her resultant morbidity. In Verena's powerlessness Olive finally reads the full dimensions of her own. In a certain sense, of course, Verena has far more power than either Olive or Ransom, and their interest in her is predicated on that fact. Both of them want to get hold of her talent and direct it in their own way and for their own benefit. Yet, the sharpest note in James's reflections on power and powerlessness in *The Bostonians* is struck through Verena because her power is seen to derive from those conditions which ultimately make her the most powerless of all. Verena's power is based on her charm, and her charm is based on her desire to please, which in turn is based on an absence of a strongly defined or assertive self. Her attractiveness, both physical and rhetorical, depends on the degree to which she is available for the projective fantasies of those who observe her, and that in turn depends on the instability which is the keynote to her character.

That Verena's talent, based as it is in the desire to please, affords her no meaningful form of power is made clear by the fact that her experience is one long series of exploitations. "There's money for someone in that girl," says Matthew Pardon, and everyone seems intent on getting it. She is exploited first by her father, who hopes to accomplish through her his heart's desire of getting into the newspapers. She is exploited equally by her mother, who hopes through her to rise socially and reclaim her due position in the world. Then she becomes prey to the attentions of people like Matthew Pardon and Henry Burrage and the boys from Harvard, whose modes of exploitation differ only according to the different uses they have in mind. While Olive seeks fulfillment for Verena, however accurate or inaccurate her sense of that may be, she relies on Verena's good nature to acquiesce in her plans and to provide her with the justification and joy of her life. And, finally, there is Ransom, who is the most exploitative of all because he is the most powerful and therefore the most possessive, the one who will allow Verena the fewest deviations from his vision of what she should be.

Ironically, as James realizes, Verena's talent functions to reinforce and perpetuate the very system she is trying to change. Verena's power is in her voice, not in her words. Indeed, it is possible to be moved by her voice without ever hearing what she says. Yet, this response is congruent with Verena's own relationship to her talent. She is detached from it; she does not see it as part of herself but as something separable, a gift she can make available to whomever most wants to use it. Thus, the initial image of her as the inspired mouthpiece of her father, if literally inaccurate, is symbolically correct. But James carries out the implications of this symbolism to their bitter conclusion, for he makes it clear that Verena's success as a feminist is predicated on the degree to which she fulfills traditional expectations about the nature of women; it is, in fact, predicated on her "femininity." The image that Verena presents is no threat to the patriarchal system; indeed, that men are so comfortable with her is the best possible indication of her harmlessness. She is passive, requiring "inspiration" in order to function; she is other-directed, attuned essentially to the needs and desires of others; she is nonintellectual, at times nonrational; and she is certainly not aggressive. She is a perfect model of the Victorian version of woman as domestic songbird, a delightful voice spouting sweet nothings for the entertainment of men. This is the vision of her that smites Olive during the afternoon in Cambridge when she watches Verena prepare to give a part of her speech for the entertainment of Harvard boys. There could be no more bitter statement of the essential powerlessness of the women's movement than in the fact that its main attraction is Verena, who enters *The Bostonians* "started up" by her father and ends it silenced by Ransom.

VI

The nature of the struggle between Olive and Ransom is defined by its object, Verena, whose essence is to yield to the greatest force. By definition, whoever wins her is the most powerful. Yet Ransom's triumph is not simply the result of his power; it is the result of his power aided by the joint powerlessness of Olive and Verena. The terms of

Ransom's relation to Verena are those of his own ego; they are dominance, possession, patronization, objectification. His possessive attitude toward Verena is obvious from their first encounter, when he sees her as the object of her father's manipulations and resents this not as an intrusion on Verena but as an intrusion on his instinctively territorial vision of what he would do with her if he owned her. The anger in his reaction reflects an attitude of rivalry, and it is this attitude which, as his interest in Verena develops, produces in him the vision of himself as her savior. Ransom's goal in relation to Verena is that of absolute possession. He believes that he has a divine right to the possession of Verena's person and that attention given by her to anything other than him is an encroachment upon this right: "But he had an odd sense of having lost something in not knowing of the other girl's appearance at the Women's Convention—a vague feeling that he had been cheated and trifled with" (p. 210).

If Verena is attracted to the vision of herself that Ransom offers, James makes no attempt to soften or disguise the nature of what she is attracted to. While Ransom is forever entreating Verena to come out, he does so only in order to lead her into a world more narrow than that of Olive's parlor. The starkness, the bleakness of his material furnishings are an image for his mental housing; his mind is itself a narrow room crudely furnished with a few sticks of thought. And, as we have seen, one of the main items in that mental furniture is contempt for women. Nothing in his relation to Verena mitigates the force of this contempt. In marrying Ransom, Verena is committing herself to a view, which, when she first hears it, makes her feel "cold, slightly sick. . . . The ugliness of her companion's profession of faith made her shiver; it would have been difficult to her to imagine anything more crudely profane" (pp. 343-44).

Even more significant for what it says about Verena is

Ransom's brutality: his perfect willingness to make her unhappy if it is in his interests; his desire to wrest from her the most painful and humiliating terms of surrender; his pleasure in her pain. It is to James's considerable credit that he associates the brutality of masculinity with the excesses of power that a sexist system makes available to men, and that he realizes it can appear in the form of a "nice guy." In the scene at Harvard when Ransom seeks to drive a wedge between Verena and Olive and to create a situation in which Verena cannot help but injure her friend, James makes the following observation: "In playing with the subject this way, in enjoying her visible hesitation, he was slightly conscious of a man's brutality—of being pushed by an impulse to test her good nature, which seemed to have no limit" (p. 250). It is the perception of Verena's powerlessness, expressed in the limitless good nature that is her particular adaptation to the condition, that elicits in Ransom the desire to exhibit to its own limitless measure the brutal face of his power. The language he chooses for thinking about his relation to Verena reflects this desire:

> if he should become her husband he should know a way to strike her dumb (p. 329)

> I certainly shall spoil it if I can (p. 373)

> he didn't care for her engagements, her campaigns, or all the expectancy of her friends . . . to "squelch" all that, at a stroke, was the dearest wish of his heart. It would represent to him his own success, it would symbolize his victory (p. 405)

> to go away proved to himself how secure he felt, what a conviction he had that however she might turn and twist in his grasp he held her fast (p. 414).

That sadism which is the quintessential expression of male power (cf. Trilling's benevolent rape) emerges in full force in the final scene, when Ransom tears Verena away from Olive. Indeed, in the vision of Olive's agony Verena can read her fate should she ever decide to take a course different from that which Ransom has "traced" for her, just as in the symbolic act which he performs as he rushes her out of the hall into the dark obscurity of the night she can read the price she will have to pay for occupying his narrow world with him—the obliteration of her own identity.

James is careful to indicate that the terms of Olive's relation to Verena are similar to Ransom's. Like Ransom's, Olive's vision of Verena is characterized by romantic fantasy and projection. Like him, she sees Verena primarily in terms of her own needs and desires, and she is hardly free of the charge of egotism. Like him, she is possessive, jealous, dominating; the same metaphors are used to describe them both. Olive's character limits Verena, who has to adapt her life to the narrow confines of Olive's anxiety. And, as with Ransom, the originating and sustaining force in the relationship is Olive. Yet, while the relationships are so clearly similar, there are nevertheless significant differences which claim as large a share of James's interest as the similarities do. For one thing, it would be difficult to attribute to Olive the naked desire to make a show of force, which so clearly motivates Ransom throughout his relation to Verena and particularly in the final scene. In the first place, Olive doesn't have the power to accomplish such a demonstration; and in the second place, while her relation to Verena is characterized by a desire to dominate, it is not defined by it as Ransom's is. Indeed, given both Ransom's attitudes toward women and his essential sadism, it is hard to avoid the conclusion that his interest in Verena is the product of Olive's and that, were Verena not the object of Olive's desire, she would not be the object of his. Less love for Verena than the desire to exhibit his power and annihilate Olive is Ransom's motive, making him single Verena out from a class which he otherwise finds damnable. Thus, while the prospect of her relationship with Olive does at times frighten Verena, there is nothing in it capable of producing the feeling she has upon discovering what Ransom really thinks.

Perhaps the differences between the two relationships can be best understood by a comparison of one of the details from two similar scenes, the scene at Cambridge in which Olive extracts from Verena the promise not to marry and the scene at the end of the novel when Ransom takes Verena off. In both instances Verena is the recipient of the same symbolic gesture, but the language that describes the two acts registers subtle differences in implication and effect:

> And Olive drew the girl nearer to her, flinging over her with one hand the fold of a cloak that hung ample upon her own meager person, and holding her there with the other, while she looked at her, suppliant but half hesitating. (p. 136)

> Ransom, as he went, thrust the hood of Verena's long cloak over her head, to conceal her face and her identity. It quite prevented recognition. . . .   (pp. 463-64)

Olive's gesture is protective and binding but it is also warm and loving—she wants to keep Verena from getting cold—and the pressure she exerts on Verena to "promise" is mitigated by her suppliant posture. Ransom's gesture is solely possessive; he wishes to conceal Verena's identity so that no one other than himself can get at her, and it carries with it the implication of the obliteration of that identity.

That Olive does not dominate Verena in the way that Ransom does is, in part, the inevitable result of her relative powerlessness. As James makes clear, it is impossible for one woman to dominate another woman to the same extent that a man can, because she has neither the self-image nor the social authority to do so. Yet, the difference between Ransom and Olive also rests in a resistance within Olive to the exercise of such power, even if she were to have it. The complexity of Olive's relation to the idea of dominating Verena is developed through the matter of Verena's promise not to marry. Exacted at first as a response to Olive's immense pain and with the reward of consistent "sweetness" held out, it is retracted by Olive the following day: "You must be safe, Verena—you must be saved; but your safety must not come from your having tied your hands. It must come from the growth of your perception; from your seeing things, of yourself, sincerely and with conviction, in the light in which I see them" (p. 140). Yet, what follows this declaration suggests Olive's ambivalence: " 'Don't promise, don't promise!' she went on. 'I would far rather you didn't. But don't fail me—don't fail me, or I shall die!' " (pp. 140-41). Like Ransom, Olive wants Verena bound, but, unlike him, she wants her bound of her own free will. The degree to which this position is based on a fear that she has neither the authority to exact such a bond nor the power to enforce it if exacted, and the degree to which it is based on a perception that the quality of freedom is essential to the meaning of their relationship is clarified in the final phase of her struggle for Verena:

> She repented of it [the lost promise] with bitterness and rage; and then she asked herself, more desperately still, whether even if she held that pledge she should be brave enough to enforce it in the face of actual complications. She believed that if it were in her power to say, 'No, I won't let you off; I have your solemn word, and I won't!' Verena would bow to that degree and remain with her; but the magic would have passed out of her spirit forever, the sweetness out of their friendship, the efficacy out of their work.   (pp. 392-93)

There is one final aspect of Olive's relation to Verena which marks it off sharply from Ransom's. Despite the anguish and rage that Verena's defection produces in her, Olive can nevertheless separate Verena from herself and look at the situation from Verena's point of view. She has a conception of Verena's happiness as Verena herself might wish to interpret it. In contrast to Ransom, Olive accepts, understands, and sympathizes with the forces pulling Verena away from her and toward Ransom, and she can feel for Verena in her struggle to fight her attraction to Ransom. Like her possessiveness, Olive's egotism is qualified by love and thus she offers Verena more of a chance at personhood than Ransom does.

James is careful to make this point as he traces Verena's development through the course of her relationship with Olive. Under Olive's tutelage and influence, and as a result of the opportunities Olive opens up to her—opportunities which certainly will not be hers with Ransom and which Verena clearly enjoys—Verena has matured. The voice Ransom hears that summer night at Cape Cod is not the voice he heard two years before at Miss Birdseye's, nor is the woman who endures the long silent night of shame with Olive the girl who came the first day to get carfare and a look at Mrs. Luna. Verena has moved from an indulgent acceptance of Olive's patronage and affection to a full partnership in their relationship: "It was of no use for her to tell herself that Olive had begun it entirely and she had only responded out of a kind of charmed politeness, at first, to a tremendous appeal. She had lent herself, given herself, utterly" (p. 398).

James values the relationship between Olive and Verena. Again and again he returns to the depth of their mutual affection, the idealism behind the joint sistership of their work, the quality of beauty in their experience together. In James's hands, it becomes a fully realized relationship, and he makes us care very deeply for its fate. It is impossible not to read that fate in the metaphors of spoilage which dominate the final pages of the novel. The vision of Ransom as a spoiler, breaking in upon an idyll and disrupting the fabric of a beautiful life, is central to James's description of those final events.

It is obvious, then, that *The Bostonians* is not a fairy tale about a wicked witch, a damsel in distress, and a heroic prince who saves her in the nick of time. On the contrary, *The Bostonians* is more nearly a tragedy in which something beautiful is seen as inevitably doomed. The massive fatalism behind the novel is most fully expressed in Verena's ultimate yielding to Ransom. James's plot supports Ransom's vision of the way things are, and his tone supports Olive's sense of the horror of this fact. Thus, Ransom is born to victory and to power, Olive and Verena to weakness and defeat, because this is the way things are and always will be. And things are this way and always will be because there is such a thing as a masculine nature and a feminine nature which no movement in the world can change. If Ransom is quintessentially masculine in his desire to "press, to press, always to press" and Verena quintessentially feminine in her desire to please, and if these things are unchangeable facts, then women are indeed doomed to be exploited and their talents doomed to be lost to the general good and swallowed up in the private service of the individual male.

But the vision that results from James's fatalism is even more bitter than this. It is not simply that women are doomed to yield to men; they are doomed to find their fulfillment and their happiness in so yielding. Verena yields to Ransom mainly because it is he alone who is capable of arousing her sexually. If women respond to male sexuality only when it is expressed in terms of power, aggression, and sadism, then the force of their sexuality is set squarely against their emancipation and their condition is hopelessly static and self-destructive. Women are doomed to be masochists whose only mode of experiencing pleasure is in the midst of pain: "she felt that to throw herself into his life (bare and arid as for the time it was),

was the condition of happiness for her, and yet that the obstacles were terrible, cruel" (p. 397). For Verena to go off with a man who despises women, whose view of things makes her sick, and who wishes to obliterate her identity is an act of masochism parallel to Olive's hurling herself upon the massed rage of the Boston audience. Indeed, James suggests, as he did with Mrs. Tarrant, that Olive and Verena are finally far more united in their common experience as women than they are separated by their differences as individuals. And what is that experience? "I shall see nothing but shame and ruin" (p. 412). Women are doomed to betray each other out of their need for those men who, because all power is vested in them, can set the terms of their various surrenders. Their common experience is suffering and shame: "it was a kind of shame, shame for her weakness, her swift surrender, her insane gyration, in the morning. . . . Distinctly, it was a kind of shame" (p. 425).

In some respects James's story is thoroughly conventional. He invokes the conventional romantic pattern of the pursuant male and the yielding female. And he invokes heavily conventional assumptions about masculine and feminine nature. But James is not conventional in his assessment of what this material means. He is not dealing in the conventional sophistries of the mystique of feminine fulfillment, the joy which inevitably results from being mastered, dominated, or "ransomed." His view of the fate of women is poignant in the extreme; and while he may assert that it is indeed their fate, he does not assert that it is good. Despite his fatalism James conveys the sense that there is something radically wrong with the way things are, that there is something grotesque about a system in which women's place is but a trivial "detail," to be lightly dismissed after a few jokes: " 'And those who have got no home (there are millions, you know), what are you going to do with *them*? . . . 'Oh,' said Ransom, 'that's a detail! And for myself, I confess, I have such a boundless appreciation of your sex in private life that I am perfectly ready to advocate a man's having a half a dozen wives' " (p. 344). By consistently locating the reforming impulse in women, James focuses attention on women's sense of uselessness, on their need to justify their existence through lives of service, and on the larger question of what women are to do with themselves and their energy—that energy which is expressed so profusely and ineffectually in the women's movement as James presents it, which issues forth in Verena's eloquence, which turns in on itself in Olive's tortured intensity, which fires the obsessive professionalism of Dr. Prance and the odysseys of Miss Birdseye, which expresses itself in the restlessness of those women who seek out the "services" of a charlatan like Selah Tarrant. It is an energy for which Ransom's system has no place, dealing with it only by stifling and paralyzing it.

While the most James can finally do in response to the suffering he so clearly perceives is to adopt the more subtle sexism of romanticizing it, celebrating it, and elevating it to the stature of the tragic, there is nevertheless a revolutionary message latent in *The Bostonians*. In the character of Olive, James has grasped, regardless of whether he knew it or not and regardless of what he felt about it, the central elements of a radical feminism. Olive's feminism is based on her perception that men constitute a class whose individual differences count for very little in comparison with their similarities. And it is based on her lesbianism, her desire to make her primary commitments to other women. Implicit in the character of Olive is the recognition that lesbianism is a key issue in feminism because in the lesbian the private and the public—those two spheres which Ransom above all wants to keep separate for women—are brought together, and in the lesbian the formidable power of woman's sexuality is set not *against* but *for* herself. In the fate of Olive and Verena one can read the central tenets of radical feminism: women will never be free to realize and become themselves until they are free of their need for men, until they know that their basic bonds are with each other, and until they learn to make a primary commitment to each other rather than to the men who would so basely ransom them.

AN AMERICAN DREAM
"Hula, Hula,"
Said the Witches

I

So it is that at the climax of the novel, when the two teenagers hike up into the Arctic Circle, we come upon one of the most sensational visions of the Absolute in American literature since the closing page of *The Narrative of Arthur Gordon Pym of Nantucket,* a delirious hallucination in which the entire Arctic Circle is revealed as the "Magnetic-Electro fief of the dream," as one immense psychic crystal, receiving into itself and storing up and retransmitting all the vibrations and lusts and instincts, all the noxious energies generated out of the daily routine and frustrations of the inhabitants of the North American continent and then flushed back to them in the form of unclean dreams and unconscious impulses. It is, in short, for the body of the globe itself, something comparable to Mailer's vision of the psychic economy of the individual body.[1]

Jameson's interpretation of *Why Are We in Vietnam?* provides a model for our reading of *An American Dream.* As the Arctic Circle is to the global body and the cancer cell to the human body, so is *An American Dream* to the body of sexual

politics: it is the repository of all the hates and fears, the
lies and disguises, the violence and cruelty, the guilt and
dread that are at the heart of sexist society; it is the unclean
dream generated by centuries of patriarchy. It is sexism
gone berserk in a metaphoric frenzy whose violent
efflorescence depends on the rich context of cultural
mythology from which it draws. It reads like an elaborate
exegesis of everything that has preceded it; its echoes are
endless. In *An American Dream* the equation, inherent in
the system of sexual politics, of love with war and sex with
power is so complete there is not even the pretense of
romance left. As Jameson puts it, in Mailer's work "sex . . .
always stands . . . for power relationships, for imposing
your own ego; and it is the vital locus of the things that can
happen to your ego when you lose, so that in this world
ego-damage is translated into sexual malfunction."[2] And
the parallel equation of the "you" with the male is also
complete. In *An American Dream* there is no suggestion that
women are people; they are utterly OTHER, the Enemy,
that against which "you" define "yourself."

Mailer, of course, makes a fetish of being male; but what
gives his fetishism its unique quality is the fact that it is
impossible to determine to what degree it is parody and to
what degree it is endorsement. Mailer is the embodiment
of what he criticizes and the criticism of what he embodies.
Having become, in effect, a male impersonator, Mailer
suggests nothing so much as a fanatical, last-ditch effort to
revive the unrevivable and save the unsavable, "a way of
extracting some vitality, like clotting blood, from defunct
opinions."[3] Mailer hides in his prose like an endangered
species in its vanishing wilderness, making the act of criticism a game of hide and seek. Everything becomes its opposite, which in turn becomes its opposite, and analysis is
unbelievably involuted and frustrating. The self-protective
intention of these stylistic gambits is obvious, but the final
result of his endless circling and covering is that he be-

comes trapped in his own escape routes. "It is as though
. . . Mailer had chosen not to repudiate the dominant value
but rather to adopt it with the fanatical exaggeration of the
newly converted, to live it to its ultimate existential limits
. . . giving his own personality over to a kind of symbolic
possession by what would otherwise look like an alien
force, transforming his life and work into a sacred reenactment of what cannot apparently be exorcized any
other way."[4]

A great purveyor of existential courage, Mailer is unwilling to face the real dread involved in relinquishing the
character structure of machismo; he is unwilling to confront the terror inherent in any genuine cultural
revolution—that terror which is the subject of Mary Daly's
Beyond God the Father and which she sees as structuring the
lives of contemporary feminists who do indeed confront
it—which requires that one die to one form of the self and
be reborn to another. And so he elaborates false dreads in
order to obscure the real dread and fills his world with the
mythology of female power and male powerlessness, with
castrating bitches, teethed wombs, murderous females,
and delicate erections forever in danger of being destroyed. What he presents, finally, is the image of a mind
increasingly dependent on its own sickness, "the plight of a
man whose powerful intellectual comprehension of what is
most dangerous in the masculine sensibility is exceeded
only by his attachment to the malaise."[5]

Mailer's work represents an end point beyond which
sexism cannot go without becoming, in ironic fidelity to the
logic of his own style, its opposite; thus, he provides the
logical conclusion for this study. Adherence to the patriarchal system and to the mythologies of male
chauvinism becomes in Mailer's hands a kind of inverted
feminism. At once the most blatantly and committedly
chauvinist of the writers studied, Mailer is also the most
subintentionally feminist. By a slight readjustment his

work can be read as a manifesto for revolutionary feminism. Through his relentless presentation of the nightmare content of the system of sexual politics and through his decision to embrace that content, to live it out to its ultimate conclusion, and to make of it the stuff of moral courage, he provides nausea enough to clear out all our pipes. And while the game he plays is designed to serve the interests of male power, it can quite easily be turned back upon itself and made to give evidence and justification and strategy for the ending of that power once and for all. If the drama that *An American Dream* records, in an endlessly involuted sequence of parody and commitment, is a struggle for male survival predicated on the twin myths of male powerlessness and female power and made possible by a male take-over of female power, then the drama of feminist criticism is the effort to straighten out those involutions, expose those myths, make clear their intent, and in so doing reclaim some of the power they have taken from women. It is an effort to take over Mailer's vision so that the action that vision leads to will not be more murder of women by men, but rather will be women's resistance to being used and abused by power masquerading as weakness. It is an effort to counter Mailer's design for exorcizing women by exorcizing him. If successful, we will have created the conditions for real courage and for the birth of something genuinely new.

II

An American Dream is "Rip Van Winkle" one hundred and fifty years later. The fantasy is the same, the plot slightly different. Nature has disappeared, time has accelerated, and women are perceived as much too threatening to go to sleep on. They cannot be allowed to die a "natural" death, to self-destruct like Dame Van Winkle while the male protagonist takes time off in nature. Rather, they must be killed and killed violently and thoroughly and again and again before the hero is able to break free and head for the West. No longer is the ideal community one's home village conveniently simplified. Instead, the place where one can finally be free to be oneself is moved farther and farther away—now somewhere in Yucatán or in the jungles of Guatemala, where there awaits a single, unidentified, though clearly male, friend. And no longer can the drama of a male take-over of female power be relegated to the realm of epigraph and footnote or be dealt with by delicate innuendo. In *An American Dream* this drama has moved to center stage and has become the central imaginative act of a novel whose protagonist operates out of the dread incurred by his fantasy of feasting on the corpse of his dead wife.

Along with the increased violence in the form the fantasy takes goes an increased commitment to making the fantasy literal, programmatic—to making it describe and prescribe a desirable mode of behavior. Despite its potential effect on the imagination and therefore the behavior of its reader, "Rip Van Winkle" is obviously a fantasy, one that presents itself as the material of a daydream on a somnolent sunny afternoon, and that at some level gently mocks the very wish to which it gives voice. But *An American Dream,* however fantastic it may appear, is not simply that. Although by no means a realistic novel, it is much too well grounded in the details of social reality to be seen as purely the design of fantasy. It at once refers to reality and seeks to affect it. One of the features of Mailer's evasive style of parodic commitment and committed parody, as expressed in both his art and his life, is that through his art he seeks to explore that curious and shadowy ground where symbol meets act and metaphor merges into reality. An example of this exploration can be seen in the potential interconnections between his essay of 1957 entitled "The White Negro," his attack on his second wife in November of 1960, and his writing of *An American Dream* in 1964-65. "The White Negro" is an exhortation to encourage the psychopath in oneself and to commit murder, if necessary, as that act of courage which alone will free one into creation and into love. Mailer's stabbing of his wife, Adele Morales, in the afterhours of a cocktail party may be seen as the inevitable acting out of that essay—the act required to make the essay more than just a word game or an extended metaphor. And the essay must be proved to be more than just a word game, because a "revolution in consciousness" must be made of firmer stuff than the cheat of language characteristic of those worlds of presidential campaigns and advertising slogans that he so consistently mocks and exposes. If Mailer wishes to moralize violence and to make it function in the service of social health, and if he sees the courage to do this as the requisite act that will save our national life from our national cancer, then of course he must have that courage of his convictions. So he stabs his wife as proof of his honesty and his courage, as a demonstration of his "pride . . . that as a sane man I can explore areas of experience that other men are afraid of."[6]

Yet, the nature of the act which is the inevitable result of the essay is significant. The choice of weapon (a penknife), of time and place (his apartment with someone else in it), and of form (two or three thrusts in the front and back, near the heart but not in it) all define the attack as symbolic of violence rather than as an attempt to murder which failed. To kill is easy enough; if murder were the aim, there would be no need for a near miss. But the crucial feature of Mailer's act is its near-miss quality, for its form is its content. The act is an exploration into that narrow territory—the territory symbolized in *An American Dream* by Kelly's parapet—where the metaphoric and the literal almost touch; it is an act which stops just short of that point where the metaphoric is transformed into the literal. The reason for this ultimate drawing back is clear; once the transformation has taken place, the nature of the act is changed and control over its meaning is lost. The symbolic act becomes the property of those institutions endowed with the authority for responding to "aberrant" and "antisocial" behavior. The murderer is judged insane and/or is incarcerated. Mailer's horror upon being arrested and sent to Bellevue for observation was that he might be seen as merely insane and therefore lose control over the meaning of his action. Above all, Mailer wanted to retain control of the situation so that he might make clear the relationship between his action and his vision of the function of the artist as a purveyor of social health. For, as art merges into action, so action merges into art, and the result is *An American Dream*, whose metaphoric frenzy seems like the afterbirth of an aborted action, as if metaphor expands in precisely the degree to which action has been limited.

But who can predict where the process stops? If, as George Schrader claims, "Mailer seems clearly to believe that in order to present such a radical possibility in the form of art one must first have experienced it oneself,"[7] surely the converse is equally true: to present "some solitary human possibility of choice which goes a little further, a little deeper, into the mysteries of the self than the last writer before him"[8] is to present a model for human behavior that extends beyond the experience of reading the novel. What is to prevent us from seeing *An American Dream* as a blueprint for murder more serious than "The White Negro" because it rides on the energy generated by that essay and its subsequent events? In *An American Dream*, murder is presented as inherently valuable and is accorded cosmic significance in Rojack's struggle to free himself from the forces of evil. Further, Mailer locates his courage as a writer and a man in the fact that he was able to let his hero kill his wife in the first installment of an eight-part serial: "[it] is like taking off your clothes in Macy's window. What do you do next? But finally I realized I was the one man in America who could do it. The clue to me is, I figure I've got as much physical courage as the next guy, but I'm profoundly afraid of being a moral coward."[9] It is Mailer's triple commitment to specifying, moralizing, and actualizing his fantasies of violence which constitutes his unique signature as a writer and his unique artistic relation to the system of sexual politics. But although this commitment presents itself as the epitome of moral courage, it hardly deserves that accolade. It is possible that Mailer's decision to begin his novel with the kind of crisis usually reserved for a conclusion is an act of courage, though some novels do it. But there is no courage involved in his choice of crisis, just as there is no courage involved in the symbolic act of stabbing his wife; it is the epitome of the ordinary and the expected, a mere repetition of the fantasy of "Rip Van Winkle" and elaborated throughout our literature and our culture. This confusion of the thoroughly conventional with the morally courageous is endemic to Mailer's work, making him fulfill his own worst fears about himself. His refusal to contemplate any cure for the sickness itself is finally an act of profound moral cowardice.

Yet, his decision to become his sickness, to be hyperviolent in a violent culture and hypermale in a sexist one, provides the conditions for an analysis of that sickness and for the realization of genuine courage. Although an essay like "The White Negro" is an apotheosis of sexism, seeking to cure sickness with sickness, it can, if one reads it as a feminist and makes some simple substitutions, become revolutionary. Every word of this essay speaks with unerring clarity and immense power to the woman who has just realized the impact of sexism in her life and who is struggling to overcome that "stench of fear" which is the product of "years of conformity and depression" and who is fighting to gain "the courage to be an individual, to speak with one's own voice."[10] Such a woman is, in fact, the essay's ideal reader, for it is she who must confront the single most oppressive and totalitarian institution in all of human culture, the concept of "masculine" and "feminine," and it is she who is most flooded by anxiety, who feels at once hopelessly schizophrenic and psychopathic and who is desperately seeking means for changing her nature. The imperative to encourage the psychopath in oneself and to set out on that uncharted journey into the rebellious imperatives of the self is directed to her deepest need. Indeed, "The White Negro" leads more logically to the symbolic act of Mailer's wife's stabbing him than to his stabbing her.

The truth of this assertion, and thus of Mailer's ironic affinity with revolutionary feminism, can be seen if we examine the contemporary event that most closely parallels Mailer's stabbing of his wife: Valerie Solanas' shooting of Andy Warhol on June 3, 1968. The analogues between these two events are considerable and fascinating. Having written the *S.C.U.M. Manifesto,* in which she postulates the necessity of eliminating men, Solanas accompanies Warhol into the office of his Factory and shoots him. Like Mailer, she is living out her exhortation, carrying through the implications of her language, translating her metaphors into action. Yet, like him, she stops short of completing the transference and rests in the middle ground of symbolic action. Solanas shoots Warhol the same number of times that Mailer stabs his wife, but she does not kill him as she so easily could have. Like Mailer, she takes a risk, but it is a closely calculated one which would seem to have its investment in exploring that narrow territory where the metaphoric approaches the literal without quite becoming it. Her commitment is not to the violent fact of murder but to the symbolic act of violence—as the necessary outgrowth of her *Manifesto* and of her personal life, as a statement of women's rage and a warning to the male establishment, and as a signal to other women to contact and express their rage. Later she comments, "I'm over it now, in any case; I don't have to do it again."[11] Not only are the source and nature of her action analogous to Mailer's, but so also is her response to the consequences of it. Like him, she fiercely resists the attempt of institutions to take over her action and co-opt its significance: she refuses the services of a lawyer, explaining that, since the charges are serious, she wants the matter "to stay in competent hands"; she objects to being dismissed as insane, saying, "It's not often that I shoot somebody. I didn't do it for nothing."[12] And, like Mailer, she makes a direct and public connection between her writing and her action, planning to submit the S.C.U.M. Manifesto as testimony in her defense, her legal brief as it were. There is no better example of Mailer's hipster than Solanas. And there is no better evidence of the self-obsessed and therefore self-destructive nature of Mailer's vision, his commitment to curing sickness with sickness, than in the fact that such an example is inconceivable to him.*

---

*The sexism in our society is demonstrated by a comparison of the newspaper and journal accounts of the two events and by a comparison of the legal and institutional treatment of the two attackers. As one might predict, in both cases the male figure received the lion's share of journalistic sympathy and interest. While it is obvious that those features of Mailer's act which make it interesting and which elicit a desire to understand him are equally applicable to Solanas, in the journalistic accounts of her attack on Warhol the focus was invariably on him and she remained a shadowy, almost unidentified, figure in the background. And while Mailer emerged from his seventeen days of observation in Bellevue protesting that "as silly and stupid as society is, it does take care of you. The awful thing was that Bellevue wasn't awful" and lamenting that "if it had been a Dickensian hell hole, I'd have come out stronger than ever but I came out prematurely temperate," Solanas was declared incompetent to stand trial and was committed for four months to the Mattawan State Hospital for the criminally insane, a Dickensian hell hole far beyond Mailer's imaginings. Mailer's wife refused to press charges, so he was given a suspended sentence and put on probation; Solanas, after release from Mattawan, was jailed in lieu of $50,000 bail and was finally sentenced to a jail term of up to three years.

There is, however, another dimension to Mailer's affinity with feminism. Read side by side, *An American Dream* and the *S.C.U.M. Manifesto* appear to be parallel documents. Both are concerned with the nature of male experience and with what it means to be male. While Solanas responds to the implications of her vision by saying "eliminate," and Mailer responds by saying "find a way to survive at any cost," the results of their parallel investigations are essentially the same. Both of them agree that men are a fragile, endangered, and hence dangerous species. Mailer, of course, does not want to be held accountable for this vision. The question of his belief is always subject to doubt and is endlessly protected by his evasive style. Yet, his investment in the exploration of that thin line between metaphor and action, like his investment in the style of evasion, commits him to a final loss of control over the meaning of his work. If the metaphoric frenzy of *An American Dream* leads toward the act of murder, it is not at all certain who it is that may be led to murder whom. The *S.C.U.M. Manifesto* can be read as a gloss on *An American Dream*; *An American Dream* can be adduced as supporting evidence for the position formulated in the *S.C.U.M. Manifesto*. In making men's violence toward women the center of his work, Mailer is also creating the conditions for the expression of women's violence toward men.

III

An American Dream is saturated with images of massive male power conglomerates. There is the Mafia, the C.I.A., the police force, the institutions of government and big business, the media networks, the university establishment; and behind them all, ensconced in his phallic tower, is Barney Kelly, the empire builder, the ultimate symbol of

conglomerate and institutional power. The book is saturated as well with images of individual men enacting violence on women: Rojack's murder of Deborah; the marine
who smashes his wife's head with a hammer; Henry Steels,
who "shacks up with a fat broad in Queens" and "six weeks
later he kills her with a poker" (*An American Dream* [N.Y.:
Dell, 1965], p. 81); Roberts, who beats up his wife; Cherry's murder. Power, it would seem, is definitely male and
in the hands of men. Yet, Rojack's thesis about human, by
which he means male, nature is that "magic, dread, and
the perception of death" (p. 15) are the sources of motivation and that cowardice is the root of neurosis—hardly a
thesis one would expect from someone in a position of
power. Indeed, *An American Dream* can be read as an elaboration of the same male fantasy that generates the critical
interpretation of *The Bostonians* and that is the opposite of
the social reality James presents in his novel. Mailer's
fantasy of female power and male powerlessness is remarkably similar to the phallic critics' mythology of an
embattled male, suffused with fear, fighting off the malign
influence of witchy, bitchy women. The function of this
mythology is nonetheless clear: it serves to disguise and
hence to perpetuate the very reality it inverts.

Our first view of Rojack is emblematic: he is hanging
from the balustrade of a balcony ten stories above the
street, only the tenuous grip of the four fingers of his right
hand between him and the itch to jump. A sense of precarious existence is Rojack's primary self-definition. Everything he experiences in the course of his thirty-two-hour
dream/nightmare is seen as a test whose passing will once
again establish for a brief period of time the fact of his
existence. The climax of the book is the most elaborate
expression of the precarious nature of Rojack's identity
and existence. His trip around the parapet of Kelly's balcony is strikingly metaphoric, presenting the image of
someone delicately poised between life and death and

alternately threatened and supported by forces outside himself. Rojack's existence is never a given; rather, it is something that must be continually proven, asserted, created. In the simplest terms he belongs to those who must become, as opposed to those who simply are.

In Rojack's obsession with death we feel the full force of his self-definition. It is not accidental that the memory that precedes his initial dangling is that of four Germans under a full moon, dying at his hand. The vision behind the eyes of the fourth soldier which plunges Rojack into a "private kaleidoscope of death" is not simply that death is "a creation more dangerous than life," but that he, Rojack, is an agent of death and that death alone is his mode of creation and source of power (p. 14). Rojack's paradigm of self is, after all, "I was: murderer," and it is this vision of himself that sets him to walk the streets of Harlem at night in search of a death that will accord with it (p. 123).

Rojack does not, however, simply fear a definition of the self as an agent of death. More significantly, he fears that he may in fact be already dead: "Instinct was telling me to die. . . . 'You can't die yet,' said the formal part of my brain, 'you haven't done your work.' 'Yes,' said the moon, 'you haven't done your work but you've lived your life, and you are dead with it.' 'Let me be not all dead,' I cried to myself" (p. 19). The evidence on the side of the moon, though, is frightening, for Rojack is permeated by a sense of emptiness at his center, a conviction that his personality is "built upon a void" (p. 14). Overwhelmed by the feeling of not belonging to himself but of being moved in on and possessed by forces outside of and distinct from himself, he comes to believe that his mind and body are in fact the agents of some alien power.

Barney Kelly elicits this fear acutely. No matter where Rojack goes, he discovers that Kelly has been there first and has in effect displaced him; and he comes to feel that he is simply acting out Kelly's desires and is being manipulated by him. The sense of displacement dominates the events surrounding his murder of Deborah. What began as a private act, born out of the imperatives of the self, rapidly becomes a public one involving the intricacies of international espionage, the relations of TV program producers to network establishments, and the internal politics of universities. When Rojack leaves his apartment building, he is surrounded by newspaper reporters; when he enters the police station, his individual act becomes lost in the power games being played there. His final release from the police has nothing to do with him or his vision of the meaning of his act but is instead a result of behind-the-scenes manipulation stemming from Kelly's belief that Rojack has done a job for him.

It is women, however, who most clearly and consistently elicit Rojack's sense of himself as marginal, threatened, and given over to death. The voice that speaks to him from the moon and tells him he is already dead is female; and it is this same voice that urges him to give himself up, confess to the murder of Deborah, and die. It is in the presence of Cherry, on the edge of their first lovemaking, that he thinks, "when I was in bed with a woman, I rarely felt as if I were making life, but rather as if I were a pirate sharpening up a raid on life, and so somewhere inside myself—yes, *there* was a large part of the fear—I had dread of the judgment which must rest behind the womb of a woman" (p. 115). In killing Deborah he fulfills his worst fears about himself; and the evil eye of her mangled corpse throws back upon him a frightening judgment. Women also confront Rojack with the fear that he has no center and is not in possession of himself. The impulse to kill Deborah begins in his sense that she has "opened a void": "I thought again of the moon and the promise of extinction which had descended on me. . . . I was now without a center. Can you understand? I did not belong to myself any longer. Deborah had occupied my center" (p. 32). Later, he has a similar experience with Cherry: "And that sensation of not belonging to myself, of being owned at my center by Deborah—that emotion which had come on me not five minutes before I killed her—now came back" (p. 166).

This ability in women to elicit such a vision of the self has its source in the belief that women are ultimately more powerful than men. Rojack is convinced that the real power behind those institutions which dominate the landscape of *An American Dream* is, in fact, female and that the ultimate manipulations are carried out not by men but by women. It is Mrs. Roosevelt who is mentioned as Stephen's mentor and entrée into the world of politics; and it is Deborah and her coterie of female friends who, on being rebuffed by Shago Martin, determine his fate by making sure that he is "no longer in danger of developing into a national figure" (p. 172). On reading the list in the society-page obituary of the organizations to which Deborah belonged, Rojack reflects on "that endless stream of intimate woman's lunches into which she disappeared every perfumed noon over the years—what princes must have been elected, what pretenders guillotined, what marriages turned in their course. . . . What a garroting must have been given my neck by the ladies of those lunches, those same ladies or their mothers who worked so neatly to make me a political career all eighteen years ago" (p. 129).

Even Kelly, that ultimate symbol of conglomerate male power, is seen by Rojack as living under the shadow of the power of women—not simply in relation to Deborah and her posthumous capacity to embarrass him with the consequences of her amateur games of espionage, but, more significantly, in relation to Ruta, who alone seems to have the kind of knowledge that can control Kelly's behavior. This vision of the relationship between male and female power is registered for Rojack, appropriately enough, as he enters the Waldorf Towers on his way to see Kelly:

"The street outside the side entrance was decked, however, with three limousines double-parked and a squad of motorcycle policemen stood at the door. . . . in the foyer . . . still another eight, each man more than six feet two, handsome as a prize herd of test-tube bulls. . . . some woman of huge institutional importance was about to descend" (pp. 193-94). The image of men as superstuds lined up in attendance on the demands of women, who represent and possess ultimate power, is central to the mythology of *An American Dream*.

This view generates Rojack's attraction to Deborah. Rojack sees Deborah, as Gatsby sees Daisy, not as a person but as a status symbol and a way into power. The need to establish his own credentials in relation to her is immediately apparent and reflects that precarious sense of identity, an identity on the make, which characterizes Rojack. And it is equally apparent that one of the ways in which his identity gets made is by his "making it" with powerful women; the "success" of the evening depends not simply on accomplishing the seduction but on who it is that one has seduced. What makes Deborah a worthy conquest and the evening "fair" is the fact that she is rich and powerful, she is Barney Kelly's daughter and a Caughlin Mangaravidi to boot, and she is sophisticated to the point of being bored by the offerings of even such extraordinary males as Jack Kennedy and Scott Fitzgerald. In seducing her Rojack proves that he is a very special "sword" indeed.

Throughout their relationship Rojack views Deborah through the lens of the status he gets from his relation to her and the power to which she provides access: "I had . . . become the husband of an heiress"; "I finally had been the man whom Deborah Caughlin Mangaravidi Kelly had lived with in marriage, and since she'd been notorious in her day, picking and choosing among a gallery of beaux . . . she had been my entry to the big league"; "I had also the secret ambition to return to politics. . . . With her beside me, I had leverage, however, I was one of the more active figures of the city—no one could be certain finally that nothing large would ever come from me" (pp. 15, 23, 23-24).

But it is not simply that Deborah represents institutional power or provides access to political power. She is also connected intimately to Rojack's capacity to realize personal power. She is the "armature" of his ego, and he fears that he does not have the "strength to stand alone" without her: "when she loved me . . . her strength seemed then to pass to mine and I was live with wit, I had vitality, I could depend on stamina, I possessed my style. . . . The instant she stopped loving me . . . why then my psyche was whisked from the stage and stuffed in a pit" (p. 24). Rojack accords Deborah complete control over his sense of who and what he is; he sees her as able to make him or break him, able to free him into power or reduce him to nothing. That Deborah possesses the key to his self-image is made clear from the start of their relationship: "'You're not Catholic, are you?' 'No.' 'I was hoping perhaps you were Polish Catholic. Rojack, you know.' 'I'm half Jewish.' 'What is the other half?' 'Protestant. Nothing really.' 'Nothing really,' she said. 'Come, take me home.' And she was depressed" (p. 37). While Rojack later attributes this depression to Deborah's conviction that he lacks a sense of grace, it seems more likely, given the way he records the interchange, that he believes her depression stems from his failure to live up to her conception of somebody interesting, from her sense of him as nothing. In contrast to her rich identity as Deborah Caughlin Mangaravidi Kelly, her efforts to get an identity out of his name result in "nothing really." It is this view of himself as nothing that Deborah continually aggravates by saying he is nothing but a bully or nothing but a coward, by reminding him that he is not her father or her first husband or her real lover. The potential for murder in Rojack's relation to Deborah is thus double: she both represents his way of becoming something and confirms his sense of being nothing.

The attribution to women of power over male self-image structures Rojack's relation to Cherry. He seeks in her, as he did in Deborah, some image of the self that will give him power and control. It is his desire to look good in Cherry's eyes and to live up to what he thinks she sees in him that enables him to resist the temptation to give in to the police and thus confirm that sense of self he fears. Cherry is directly responsible for his "salvation," as Deborah is for his damnation. But the point is still the same; Rojack needs from Cherry exactly what he needed from Deborah and killed her for not providing. His identity and his power are inextricably connected to women. Women are the arbiters of his fate.

What fuels Rojack's conviction that women are in control of his life is a mythology which pervades *An American Dream* and which posits as its central premise the belief that women, as a result of being women, are in possession of an elemental power of which their institutional, political, and personal power is but a sign. *An American Dream* is grounded in the mystique of women as "psychic." Good, blonde Cherry is psychic enough to know who is going to win at the gambling tables of Las Vegas, and she is able to beat out a Mafioso by playing on his fear that she will haunt him. Herself a potential killer, Cherry has acquired the kind of power that can get people killed. Possession of psychic powers is central to Kelly's Bess: "Each time we got together I felt as if I were an open piggy-bank: had to take whatever she would drop into me; her coin was powers. My nose for the market turned infallible" (p. 228). The connection between women's possession of psychic powers and their access to institutional, political, and personal power is revealed in Bess, for it is her psychic powers that put her in a position to control not only the stock market but also Kelly: "I was in her damn grip. Intolerable. I was afraid of her. More afraid of her than I'd been of anybody" (p. 228).

Rojack and Deborah double Kelly and Bess: "She had powers, my Deborah, she was psychic to the worst degree, and she had the power to lay a curse" (p. 27). Deborah's possession of psychic powers defines her as it defines Rojack's relation to her, creating his sense of being in her control, of acting in response to impulses, messages, and commands from her, a puppet on the end of her invisible strings. What Deborah's witchcraft controls, though, is not just Rojack's behavior: "Yes, I had come to believe in grace and the lack of it, in the long finger of God and the swish of the devil, I had come to give my scientific apprehension to the reality of witches" (p. 38). Deborah's power is great enough and Rojack's precariousness great enough that she has, in effect, taken over his mind.

This mystique of women as psychic has its roots in a biological mythology that is central to the drama and the politics of *An American Dream*. According to this mythology, women's power derives from their possession of a womb, that "mysterious space within," that "purse of flesh" in which are "psychic tendrils, waves of communication to some conceivable source of life, some manifest of life come into human beings from a beyond."[13] Behind "that woman's look that the world is theirs" is the fact of their biology, which, by providing a ligature between themselves and elemental sources of power, shapes the nature of their identity (p. 48). Women have the power that derives from a fixed and stable identity, a conviction of existence, an assurance of being on the side of life. It is understandable, given this myth of biology, that Rojack's sense of his existence as precarious and of women as having power in themselves and over him should emerge most clearly in his sexual relations with them. Rojack's vision of the way women use sex is that of the "considerable first night" (p. 186) offered to a second lover as a comment on the first.

Thus, the man they are in bed with is of less importance than the man they are humiliating through the gusto of their infidelity, and the male comes off a loser no matter what his role: "Now I could know again why women never told the truth about sex. It was too abominable when they did" (p. 186). But the abominable truth that women have to tell through sex is nothing other than the fear that persistently plagues Rojack—the fear that there is nothing inside him, no center to his being; the fear that he is irrelevant and hence nonexistent; the fear that he is an agent of death rather than life. Contemplating Deborah's infidelity exposes the hollowness at his center and makes him want to jump, just as Deborah's saying she doesn't need him any more sexually sets off the murderous impulse in him.

In his relation with Cherry, Rojack articulates most clearly the connection between the nature of his sexual experience with women and his fears about his own identity: "The possibility that what I felt, when we made love, was a sensation which belonged to me alone, left me murderous" (p. 166). Behind this fear that male and female sexual experience are separate and distinct, behind the fear that he can never know whether what *he* experiences is what *she* experiences, is the fear that he is not necessary for women's sexual pleasure. The face of this fear is revealed when Cherry tells him that with him she has had for the first time an orgasm with a man inside her. Although presented as a testament to his powers, her remark has the effect of reminding him how rarely men give sexual pleasure to women and therefore of eliciting the fear that she may be lying to him and that he, like all the other men she has been with, is unnecessary for her pleasure. Only in the context of this fear can one understand the crucial importance of the vaginal orgasm in Rojack's sexual mythology.

Rojack's sense of irrelevance which produces in him the fear of being an agent of death who may be already dead is not limited to his questions about his role in women's sexual pleasure. He is further terrified by the thought that he is not necessary for creation. The belief that women have the capacity for self-generated reproduction has long been a phantom of the male imagination, appearing in modes as disparate as the elaborate mythology surrounding the Virgin Mary and the slang phrase, "she's gotten herself pregnant." What gives weight to this fear is the inescapable fact that no man can ever know for certain that he is the father of any woman's child; paternity is at best a hypothesis. Rojack's obsession with paternity—his hatred of devices of contraception, his refusal to make love to Cherry until she has removed her diaphragm, his horror at the idea that she aborts her child because she does not know whether the father is Shago or Tony—both points to this fact and seeks to compensate for and overcome it. In this fact are the origins of that quality of mystery which Rojack feels to be women's nature, and which makes him hate and fear them, for all other unknowings are avatars of this one: "he said, 'Did you know she did some work for us?'—said it in such a way I would never know for certain, not ever, there was something in his voice I could not for certain deny" (p. 246).

The sexual dimension of the paradigm that men become and women are reinforces the biological context of the myth of woman's power and man's powerlessness. In *An American Dream*, an identification is made between the precariousness of male existence and a precariousness in male sexuality. This connection is dramatized through the structure of Rojack's thirty-two-hour dream/nightmare. The series of tests he undergoes serves as metaphor for the supreme sexual test. The metaphor is literalized in the final test, where the question becomes, Can I get up? Rojack's walk around the parapet is a thinly veiled analogue for an erection. *The Prisoner of Sex* provides a useful gloss on the attitudes toward male sexuality in *An*

American Dream. In *The Prisoner of Sex* Mailer locates a major source of his hostility to the Women's Movement in its failure to realize "that a firm erection on a delicate fellow was the adventurous juncture of ego and courage," and in its "dull assumption that the sexual force of a man was the luck of his birth, rather than his finest moral product."[14] The same vision informs Mailer's remarks about D.H. Lawrence: "he had lifted himself out of his natural destiny which was probably to have the sexual life of a woman, had diverted the virility of his brain down into some indispensable minimum of phallic force—no wonder he worshipped the phallus, he above all men knew what an achievement was its rise from the root, its assertion to stand proud on a delicate base."[15]

This analysis of Lawrence, however, suggests another dimension to the precariousness of male sexuality: one's struggle to become male is an attempt to avoid one's natural destiny, which is to be female. The numerous references in *An American Dream*, in one form or another, to male homosexuality indicate its significance for Rojack. Yet, what is crucial here is not the degree to which Rojack may or may not have homosexual desires, but rather what he thinks it means for a male to give in to those desires. The clue is given early in Rojack's account of his killing of the German soldiers: "a great bloody sweet German face, a healthy spoiled overspoiled young beauty of a face, mother-love all over its making, possessor of that over-curved mouth which only great fat sweet young faggots can have when their rectum is tuned and entertained from adolescence on, came crying, sliding, smiling up over the edge of the hole" (p. 11). For Rojack, as for Mailer (note his remarks on Genet in *The Prisoner of Sex*), the identifying act of male homosexuality is anal intercourse and the male homosexual is a mother's boy who becomes sexually female. Male homosexuality is not seen as an equal sexual relation between two men but rather as a situation in which one man is used as a woman by another man. This attitude is, of course, the inevitable consequence of Mailer's concept of sex as solely a function of power; yet, its implications are deeper than this. In all his comments on the subject, Mailer's focus is on the man who is made a woman. Becoming female is for Mailer the essence of homosexual desire, because what male homosexuality represents for him, and consequently why it must be resisted, is the tendency in men to be women. Behind Mailer's view of male homosexuality is a conviction that the ur-state of human sexuality is female and that male sexuality is something created. Males must continually fight their way out of this state amd must continually create themselves sexually as male. Achieved against the grain, male sexuality is always in danger of ceasing to exist, "defeated by the lurking treachery of Freudian bisexuality, the feminine in a man giving out like a trick knee at a track meet."[16] Male homosexuality takes its peculiar significance from the fact that it proves the validity of the paradigm of female being and male becoming, and keeps alive the fears that are its result. The male homosexual is a man who has given in to the tendency to be female and who has as a result ceased to exist.*

That Rojack fears in himself the tendency to be sexually female and that this fear is partly the source of his dread of nonexistence are suggested in a number of ways. Consider, for instance, his predilection for analingus, an experience in which he is penetrated and hence "female." No wonder Rojack becomes murderous when Deborah reveals she has shared this practice with other men.† Or consider his peculiar susceptibility to being moved in on and pos-

---

*Mailer's work clarifies the political function of the culture's obsession with homosexuality. By keeping the image of the "faggot," the male as woman, in the forefront of cultural consciousness, he is able to justify ever greater excesses of masculinity as requisite antidotes for this induced fear.

†That analingus is the practice at issue between Rojack and Deborah is made clear from Mailer's commentary on *An American Dream* in *The Prisoner of Sex:*

sessed and his particular horror upon confronting this susceptibility in himself or other men. When Kelly describes himself as a piggy bank open to receive the coin of Bess's powers, he is presenting an image of the male as a "purse of flesh." Or consider the extraordinary violence and the nature of Rojack's attack on Shago Martin, Cherry's faintly effeminate black lover: "I took him from behind . . . and we ended with Shago in a sitting position, and me behind him on my knees, my arms choking the air from his chest as I lifted him up and smashed him down, and lifted him up and smashed him down again" (p. 181). A metaphor for homosexual rape, the attack has the function of exorcizing Rojack's fear of being female by forcing someone else to act out the homosexual possibility. In seeking to annihilate Shago, Rojack seeks to annihilate the woman in him. Significantly, it is Shago's refusal to capitulate and his final taunt that Rojack has merely "killed the little woman in me" that reopen the floodgates of dread in Rojack (p. 183).

Rojack's fear of being sexually female provides a key to understanding his mythology of women's power. If their sexuality is a given while his is something that must be continually created against it, then they have both the power which derives from simply being and the power which derives from his needing them in order to become. And it is just possible that in making love to a woman the impulse to be female is as strongly elicited as the desire to

"Still, there is a story they tell of Kate Millett when the winds blow and lamps gutter with a last stirring of the flame. Then, as the skirts of witches go whipping around the wick, they tell how Kate went up to discuss the thesis at her college and a learned professor took issue with her declaration that the wife of the hero Rojack . . . had practiced sodomy with husband and lovers. 'No, no,' cried the professor. 'I know the author, I know him well, I have discussed the scene with him more than once and it is not sodomy she practices, but analingus. It is for that she is killed, since it is a vastly more deranging offense in the mind's eye!'" (p. 71). That Deborah does it to Steve is made clear from her comment, as she informs him she will never do it with him again, that "the thought—at least in relation to you, dear sweet—makes me brush my gums with peroxide" (p. 34).

become male, so that women have at their disposal as well the power that derives from their representing his deepest, most secret, and most feared desire—to be them.

IV

One can read *An American Dream* as a series of strategies for coping with the vision of women as powerful and men as powerless, while never forgetting that this vision itself is the novel's major strategy, justifying patriarchy as survival. At the end of the book Rojack is alive and the women are dead. Rojack's strategy has two parts. One is a series of assaults on the sources of women's power and on the image of women as powerful; the other is a set of methods that enables him to redefine himself as powerful and to incorporate women's power into himself. There is one scene that contains Rojack's strategy in all its complexity. In the early hours of the morning, after leaving the police station where he has been held for questioning, Rojack goes to the club where Cherry is singing and listens to her. During one part of her act Rojack is struck by the perfection of her singing: "Cherry was singing: *When the deep purple falls over sleepy garden walls. On sleepy garden walls* she struck five perfect notes, five, like the five bells of an angel come to the wake of a bomb, clear, a cluster of the loveliest consecutive sounds I ever heard" (p. 96). In the number that follows, however, he finds himself focusing on her foot as it beats out the rhythm and observing that she has painted her toenails: "I was taken with this vanity, I was absorbed with it, for like most attractive women, her toes were the ugliest part of her body" (pp. 96-97). The perception of perfection induces the need to deflate, and Cherry's attractiveness is reduced to a parenthetical given whose significance rests in defining the form of her ugliness. Yet, Cherry's toes are ugly to Rojack because they are "greedy," "self-satisfied," and "complacent" (p. 97). In calling her vain, he is in fact registering his sense of her self-satisfaction, "that woman's look that the world is theirs."

Aware of this quality in her, he feels depressed while watching her, and he thinks automatically of death: "[I] came each instant nearer to the murmur one hears in the tunnel which leads to death" (p. 97). The vision of women's self-satisfaction and independence, rooted as it is in all the myths of female power discussed above, elicits from Rojack the corollary vision of the precarious and death-oriented nature of his own identity. But there is a pernicious twist in the formulation which grows immediately out of Rojack's intimations of death: "Women must murder us unless we possess them altogether" (p. 97). The hint of death, generated from his perception of himself, is given a specific focus, location, and agency so that his fear becomes women's murderousness. The function of this inversion is obvious—Rojack's own murderous impulses projected outward onto women become the justification for his "possessing them altogether"; thus, the impulse to suicide is transformed into the act of murder and justified as self-defense.

Rojack's capacity for such projective transformations is evident throughout the book; it is one of his major strategies for survival because it offers such immense possibilities for obscuring and thus redefining the nature of the self and its impulses. There is, for example, the moment when he returns from his sexual encounter with Ruta to confront Deborah's corpse and feels an overwhelming desire to "kill her again, kill her good this time, kill her right. I stood there shuddering from the power of this desire, and comprehended that this was the first of the gifts I'd plucked from the alley, oh Jesus, and I sat down in a chair as if to master the new desires Ruta had sent my way" (p. 52). Neatly, Rojack lays upon Ruta the burden of his own murderousness. Or, again, there is the irony that at the very moment when the police are changing their tone toward him because they have discovered that he is a war hero and a killer, he expostulates, "I had come to the conclusion a long time ago that all women were killers" (p. 81).

Projection also provides the mechanism for scapegoating. In murdering Deborah, Rojack makes her into his scapegoat and accomplishes the ritual of his own purification. The suicide Rojack nearly commits at the opening of the book is paralleled by the mock suicide he makes Deborah enact a few hours later. In effect, Deborah commits suicide for him, takes the plunge toward which he is drawn, and carries off with her the psyche that brought him to the verge; in the story that Rojack tells the police to explain Deborah's "suicide," the experience he describes is his own. Rojack locates in Deborah everything he most fears to be true of himself, and in killing her he kills that self and is reborn a new man: "my flesh seemed new"; "Deborah's dying had given me new life" (pp. 36, 91).

If Rojack is able to project his own murderous fear onto women and, in so doing, to justify as self-defense his desire to possess them altogether, he is also capable of equating women's resistance to being possessed with their being evil. At one point Rojack blames the failure of his marriage to Deborah on her tyrannical will, and to a considerable extent it is Deborah's refusal to bend her will to his that makes her evil in his eyes. Despite the fact that Cherry appears willing to be possessed—she is, after all, essentially a whore who has made her way in the world by serving men—she too finally resists being known (thus the horror for Rojack of Robert's parting taunt, "did you know she did some work for us?"), and she resists being possessed: "I had a fear now of the singer on the stand, for her face, yes, perhaps I could possess that altogether, perhaps that face could love me. But her bee-hind! of course I could not possess that ass, no one ever had, maybe no one would, and so all the difficulty had gone down to her feet, yes the five painted toes talked of how bad this girl could be" (p. 97). She is so bad that she has to die, her death being the only way she can be possessed altogether, as it is the only way Rojack can protect himself from being possessed by her. Protection is, of course, the function of this particular act of projection. Women's resistance to being possessed is evil precisely to the degree that Rojack is susceptible to being possessed by them. They must be possessed so that *he* will not be, and the fear that lies at the heart of his sense of self must be exorcized by converting what is death for him into what is good for them.

Given Rojack's vision of the nature of female sexuality, it is understandable that the evil of Cherry's resistance to being possessed should be presented in sexual terms; and it is understandable too that the aggressive impulse which inevitably follows his perception of how bad she could be is directed at her sexuality and is ultimately perceived as hers:

> I shot one needle of an arrow into the center of Cherry's womb, I felt it go in. I felt some damage lodge itself there. She almost lost her song. One note broke, the tempo shuddered, and she went on, turned to look at me then, a sickness came off her, something broken and dead from the liver, stale, used-up, it drifted in a pestilence of mood toward my table, sickened me as it settled in. And there was a touch of regret in that exhalation from her, as if she had been saving such illness in the hope she might inflict it on no one, that her pride would be to keep her own ills to herself, rather than pass them on. (pp. 97-98)

Afflicted in fact by his own sickness, Rojack once again disguises the origin of his affliction in order to purchase his survival, no matter how vicious and dishonest the terms or how precarious the ground. His act of aggression is subtly transformed as he relocates the source of injury in Cherry, who becomes the aggressor inflicting a pestilence that passes into and sickens him. In a striking act of imaginative conversion, Rojack presents himself as the conduit through whom her sickness passes and is purged. Feeling nausea "collecting in all my pipes," Rojack rushes out to vomit forth the puke of the world and thus to purify it: "if the murderer were now loose in me, well, so too was a saint of sorts, a minor saint no doubt, but free at last to absorb the ills of others and regurgitate them forth" (p. 98).

The brilliance of this strategy of conversion can be understood if we consider for a moment the implications of Rojack's presenting himself in the imagery of sainthood. First, such a conception represents a positive male self-image, one capable of being set against the imputations of a figure like Barney Kelly and capable of allaying his fears about what it means to be male. If Kelly represents what Rojack most fears becoming, the image of sainthood represents a positive possibility for the self. In the battle for Rojack's allegiance, it is father Roberts, not father Kelly, who wins and wins in part because he is an Irish cop, a member of that nation who alone "know how to cry for the dirty polluted blood of all the world" (p. 247). Second, sainthood derives from Christ and Christ derives from the processes of projection and take-over so central to Rojack's strategy for survival. Christ is the result of that ancient take-over in which male gods were substituted for female ones and female powers of creativity were accorded to male deities.[17] As the Son of God the Father, creator of the universe, whose human image duplicated the heavenly act of self-generation by giving birth to woman from his rib, Christ is at the heart of that mythology which is the ultimate strategy for rearranging reality in order to cope with the fear that women's sexuality and its implications for the nature of male identity presents. In contrast to homosexuality, it is a way in which men can become women without ceasing to be men.

The imagery Rojack uses to describe his particular version of taking upon himself the ills of others and so purifying the world reflects this process. Like the image used by Kelly to capture the essence of his psychic relation to Bess, the imagery Rojack invokes is that of a receptacle. He sees himself as impregnated with the sins of the world, and in an act analogous to childbirth he vomits the sickness forth as a creation that gives to the world new possibilities. Thus, the pattern is complete: afraid that he will be possessed and dead because he lacks that center of identity which those who are biologically creative have, and murderous as a result of his fear, Rojack projects his murderousness onto women and uses this strategically created attribution to justify his assault on them. By killing them he at once removes their threat to him and takes into himself their creative powers, able at last to become them. It is the same pattern that provides the framework for his relation to Deborah: kill, eat, incorporate, and become.

What makes Cherry good for Rojack, however temporarily, is her willingness to support this process of the male take-over of female powers. Cherry is decidedly uncomfortable with the possibilities of her own power. Like Deirdre, the other "good" female figure in the book, "a delicate haunted girl with eyes which contained a promise she would learn everything about you if she looked too long, and so chose not to look," Cherry wishes to disavow the power that has accrued to her as a result of her connection with Kelly (p. 28). She does not want to be a witch. Coming from her last number in the nightclub, Cherry sits down at the table with Rojack, who offers to recite to her his one poem: "Witches have no wit, said the magician who was weak. . . . Hula, hula, said the witches" (p. 109). Cherry responds to the poem by getting up and singing a hymn: *"Jesus saves and keeps me. / He's the one I'm waiting for. / Every day with Jesus / Is sweeter than the day before"* (p. 111). The peculiarity of her response (and it is peculiar) can be understood only if one sees it in terms of Rojack's strategies for survival. In singing a song to Christ, Cherry is making explicit her disavowal of any desire to be a witch. By celebrating the image of power as male, she is reenacting the drama of the male take-over of female power and is giving her energies to the strategies of Rojack's survival. And the particular hymn she chooses gives ample testimony of her willingness to be possessed and to the male's power to possess. It is no wonder Rojack feels she offers him the possibility of redemption.

V

Rojack's strategy for survival also involves an assault on the sources of women's power and on the image of women as powerful. This assault is carried out in a number of different ways. For example, it is important to Rojack that Deborah's spying activities be defined as essentially amateurish, at root simply sexual and motivated primarily by a desire to embarrass her father. He also takes great pleasure in mocking female magic in the form of Mrs. Tharchman and her theories about how "the last meal a person eats before they die determines the migration of their soul" (p. 138), though it is difficult to see how her theories differ from his. Similarly, he is contemptuous of Cherry's attempts to be profound on the subjects of magic, incest, and power, although her ideas seem remarkably similar to his and Kelly's, both of which are treated quite differently. His snide reference to Deborah's superficial knowledge of music trivializes her interest in Shago and reduces it to the level of the faddish and spiteful. Since Shago's music is itself a kind of magic, it is important that Deborah have no real insight into it, that it be something only he understands. And Rojack's interest in Shago's singing is, of course, increased after Shago has humiliated Deborah.

The assault on women's power is also carried out by equating women with their sexuality and then degrading that sexuality. Cherry's personality is finally in her ass, and the class differences between Ruta and Deborah are obliterated in the shared stench of their female flesh: "They were mistress and maid and put their musk in opposite pockets" (p. 54). The assault is most apparent, however, in Rojack's encounters with Ruta. When Ruta appears at the door of Kelly's suite in the Waldorf Towers, it is inevitable that Rojack will superimpose on her present sophistication the memory of "the last time I had been this close," when "Ruta's hair was half down her neck, the roots had shown, lipstick was half off her mouth, clothes up, off, to every side, her clump in my fingers" (p. 197). Equally inevitable is his belief that the worse he treats her, the better she likes it. When Rojack interrupts Ruta in the act of masturbation and proceeds to give her the "real thing," she is exposed as a Nazi pig who gets her pleasure in rooting about. The more *verboten* the act and the more deeply she resists it, the more she really wants it. In degrading Ruta, Rojack is able to make her become "mine as no woman ever had, she wanted no more than to be part of my will" (p. 48). The function of such successful degradation is obvious: it removes the fear that women's sexuality makes them independent of men by revealing them to be helpless masochists dependent upon the whims of male sadism to release them into themselves.

It is, however, in the literalizing of Rojack's imaginative wounding of Cherry's womb that the major attack on the sources of women's power and on the image of women as powerful is carried out. In reading *An American Dream,* one is confronted with a massive assault on the womb. There is not one instance of successful fulfillment of female creativity. Instead, *An American Dream* is saturated with references to wombs gone sour and dead, to the womb as "a heartland of revenge," "an empty castle," "a storehouse of disappointments," "a graveyard." Deborah has had one

child by a Caesarean section and then a miscarriage, which
"came brokenly to birth, in terror . . . of the womb which
was shaping it" (p. 31). Possessed of a malformed uterus to
begin with, Deborah is denied all possibility for another
child with this miscarriage. Ruta's womb is a graveyard
with just "one poor flower growing in a gallery," and
whenever she attempts to conceive "it burns" (pp. 48, 215).
Sterility defines Leonora, and when she finally does conceive, the birthing is again Caesarean. Cherry has had two
abortions and believes she can never have a child because
"the doctor Kelly sent me to hinted something was wrong"
(p. 167). When Cherry finally has an orgasm, which con-
vinces her she has conceived a child she could wish to bring
to term, she is flooded with the premonition of imminent
death. The connection of women's discovery of their sexuality with a conviction of death, expressed in the belief in
the "unmitigable fact that women who have discovered the
power of sex are never far from suicide" (p. 57), is part of
the pattern of projection and scapegoating. If women can
be made to express the sense of death that is in fact
Rojack's fear about his own sexuality, then they may also
be made to carry off the death wish associated with it. But
the connection is also the final phase of the assault on
women's power, for it converts the womb from creativity
and life to an agent of death. Thus, women's sexuality,
which in the mythology of An American Dream is the ultimate source of their power, is redefined and its threat
removed.

The obvious corollary to the assault on the womb is the
reassigning to men of the power robbed from women.
This reassignment is a variation on Rojack's myth of the
self as saint and is part of the drama of a male take-over of
female power. Male doctors define for a woman the state
of her uterus, her chances of conceiving or not conceiving;
they interrupt pregnancies by aborting them; or they perform Caesareans, becoming the only agent through which

the potential of women's creativity can be realized. At every stage of female creativity men intervene and redirect the power of women to themselves, becoming, in effect, the creators of female creativity. In intercourse with Ruta, Rojack changes her womb from a "deserted warehouse" to a "modest decent place" with snug walls and a sweet odor, where her "one poor flower" will have a chance at fertilization. Later, he attributes Ruta's coolness toward him to her resentment of the fact that "'you half-promised to make me a baby . . . and then you didn't'" (p. 215). Similarly, Cherry's capacity for conception is tied to an orgasm that Rojack alone can give her. In spite of great odds Kelly finally succeeds in impregnating Leonora, thereby illustrating the maxim that there is no womb so sterile that a good man can't fertilize it. That same mystique of male seed makes Ruta beg, "'Don't give all the good things to your wife'" (p. 51) and makes Rojack fear the curse from his sperm left "perishing in the kitchens of the Devil" (p. 52).

The vision of men as the creators of female creativity, the obvious salve for the fear that men are not necessary for creation, is given a final twist at the end of the book when Rojack, on first confronting Kelly's parapet, has "a sudden thought, 'If you loved Cherry, you would jump,' which was an abbreviation for the longer thought that there was a child in her, and death, *my* death, my violent death, would give some better heart to that embryo just created, that indeed I might even be created again, free of my past" (p. 210). This "sudden thought" is a compressed version of Rojack's entire mental process. It invokes that sense of self which opens the book; and it invokes his belief that death is a creation "more dangerous than life" and that in murdering Deborah he has become a participant in this negative creation. But the "sudden thought" transforms these fears and redefines the self by redefining the nature of Rojack's relation to death. In conceiving of his violent death as the way in which *he* can give birth to Cherry's child, death becomes the means for him to become an agent of life. The redefinition of the self which this "sudden thought" represents is implicit in his final musing that, were he to do this, he would become "created again, free of my past."

But Rojack finally resists the logic of his thought and rejects its conclusion. He neither takes the jump that would give heart to the embryo nor takes that second walk around the parapet, which would save Cherry's life. It is at this point that the politics of *An American Dream* become clear. Despite his posturings to the contrary, it is obvious that Rojack is in control and that his belief in male powerlessness, like his belief in female power, is conceived in the interest of perpetuating that male power whose existence is the novel's great unmentionable. *An American Dream* is generated not out of a sense of precarious identity but out of a thorough commitment to the fact of male power embedded in those images of massive power conglomerates and in the pattern of individual acts of violence. Rojack's mythology of the self romanticizes the male, legitimizes the hatred of and aggression on women, and maintains the system of male power which enacts that hatred and aggression. To the "precarious" male, forever struggling to become and forever fighting to achieve an identity, are accorded tolerance, understanding, sympathy, support, and heroic stature. One begins to realize that this vision is evolved because of its utility.

In fact, *An American Dream* makes a cult of male weakness; it is built upon a positive libido for the myth of the male as an endangered species. If men are so weak, then, of course, whatever they do to women is explicable as the simple attempt to make things equal. Such "logic" provides the perfect ground for tyranny. It is just this logic that Mailer uses in *The Prisoner of Sex* when he describes Lawrence as a man for whom "dominance over women was not tyranny but equality," or Miller as someone who "captured something in the sexuality of men as it had never been seen before, precisely that it was man's sense of awe before woman, his dread of her position one step closer to eternity (for in that step were her powers) which make men detest women, revile them, humiliate them, defecate symbolically upon them. . . ."[18] The myth of women's power, like the myth of male weakness, is clearly one of the most valuable constructs of sexual politics.

Rojack's mythology, like Mailer's style, is radically insincere. At some level Rojack recognizes the speciousness of his imaginative logic: "Witches have no wit, said the magician who was weak." To rob witches of their wit through the mythology of male weakness is not merely vicious, it is finally pathetic. No wonder Rojack dreads the judgment of women. If the history of civilization is the drama of male robbery of female power, Rojack's reenactment of that drama as myth and through myth is a version of an ancient crime. Like civilized man who has stolen the secrets of the gods, Rojack must live with the sense of "some enormous if not quite definable disaster which awaits us" (p. 150). The dread Rojack experiences is the accumulated weight of centuries of theft; it is the price he pays for his power and for the mythology which supports it. Well, "hula, hula," said the witches.

NOTES

Introduction

1. Carolyn Heilbrun, "Millett's *Sexual Politics:* A Year Later," *Aphra* 2 (Summer 1971), 39.
2. Mary Daly, *Beyond God the Father: Toward a Philosophy of Women's Liberation* (Boston: Beacon, 1973), p. 8.
3. Adrienne Rich, "When We Dead Awaken: Writing as Re-Vision," *College English* 34 (1972), 18.
4. Cynthia Ozick, "Women and Creativity: The Demise of the Dancing Dog," *Motive* 29 (1969); reprinted in *Woman in Sexist Society*, eds. Vivian Gornick and Barbara Moran (New York: Signet-New American Library, 1972), p. 450.
5. Kate Millett, *Sexual Politics* (Garden City: Doubleday, 1970), p. 58.
6. *College English* 34 (1973), 1075.
7. "Dwelling in Decencies: Radical Criticism and the Feminist Perspective," *College English* 32 (1971), 887; reprinted in *Sex, Class, and Culture* (Bloomington: Indiana University Press, 1978), p. 16.
8. *College English* 32 (1971), 855.
9. Ibid., 856-57.
10. *Massachusetts Review* 13 (1972), 226, 227.
11. *Thinking About Women* (New York: Harcourt Brace Jovanovich, 1968), pp. 149-50.
12. Edwards, p. 230.

Chapter 1

1. Philip Young, "Fallen from Time: The Mythic Rip Van Winkle," *Kenyon Review* 22 (1960); reprinted in *Psychoanalysis and American Fiction*, ed. Irving Malin (New York: Dutton, 1965), p. 23.
2. Leslie Fiedler, *Love and Death in the American Novel* (1960; rpt. New York: Meridian-World, 1962), xx-xxi.

3. Both Young, op. cit., and Henry Pochmann, "Irving's German Sources in *The Sketch Book*," *Studies in Philology* 27 (1930), 489-94, discuss at some length the heroic context of Rip's experience, which includes such figures as King Arthur, Charlemagne, and Frederick Rothbart.

4. Young, p. 29n.

5. See William Hedges, *Washington Irving: An American Study, 1802-1832* (Baltimore: Johns Hopkins Press, 1965), pp. 138-39: "The femaleness of the landscape suggests that in transferring a German folk legend to an American setting Irving has by no means obliterated all traces of the sexual fears and desires which the basic myth of a long sleep, found in many forms in many countries, usually seems to embody." Philip Young, p. 39, focusing somewhat euphemistically on the "extremely arresting" description of the terrain Rip covers in company with the little men, suggests that what Rip witnesses in the mountains is a highly disguised form of an ancient fertility rite and that Rip's sexual reluctance is revealed in the fact that he finds the little men sad and responds to their activity by going to sleep.

6. See, for example, Brooks and Warren, *Understanding Fiction* (New York: Appleton-Century-Croft, 1943), pp. 103-106: "We are not, of course, to conceive of Aylmer as a monster, a man who would experiment on his own wife for his own greater glory. Hawthorne does not mean to suggest that Aylmer is depraved and heartless. . . . Aylmer has not realized that perfection is something never achieved on earth and in terms of mortality"; Richard Harter Fogle, *Hawthorne's Fiction: The Light and The Dark*, rev. ed. (Norman, Okla.: University of Oklahoma Press, 1964), pp. 117-31; Robert Heilman, "Hawthorne's 'The Birthmark': Science as Religion," *South Atlantic Quarterly* 48 (1949), 575-83: "Aylmer, the overweening scientist, resembles less the villain than the tragic hero: in his catastrophic attempt to improve on human actuality there is not only pride and a deficient sense of reality but also disinterested aspiration"; F. O. Matthiessen, *American Renaissance* (New York: Oxford University Press, 1941), pp. 253-55; Arlin Turner, *Nathaniel Hawthorne* (New York: Holt, Rinehart, and Winston, 1961), pp. 88, 98, 132: "In 'The Birthmark' he applauded Aylmer's noble pursuit of perfection, in contrast to Aminadab's ready accep-

tance of earthiness, but Aylmer's achievement was tragic failure because he had not realized that perfection is not of this world." The major variation in these readings occurs as a result of the degree to which individual critics see Hawthorne as critical of Aylmer. Still, those who see Hawthorne as critical locate the source of his criticism in Aylmer's idealistic pursuit of perfection—e.g., Millicent Bell, *Hawthorne's View of the Artist* (New York: State University of New York, 1962), pp. 182-85: "Hawthorne, with his powerful Christian sense of the inextricable mixture of evil in the human compound, regards Aylmer as a dangerous perfectibilitarian"; William Bysshe Stein, *Hawthorne's Faust* (Gainesville: University of Florida Press, 1953), pp. 91-92: "Thus the first of Hawthorne's Fausts, in a purely symbolic line of action sacrifices his soul to conquer nature, the universal force of which man is but a tool." Even Simon Lesser, *Fiction and the Unconscious* (1957; rpt. New York: Vintage-Random, 1962), pp. 87-90 and pp. 94-98, who is clearly aware of the sexual implications of the story, subsumes his analysis under the reading of misguided idealism and in so doing provides a fine instance of phallic criticism in action: "The ultimate purpose of Hawthorne's attempt to present Aylmer in balanced perspective is to quiet our fears so that the wishes which motivate his experiment, which are also urgent, can be given their opportunity. Aylmer's sincerity and idealism give us a sense of kinship with him. We see that the plan takes shape gradually in his mind, almost against his conscious intention. We are reassured by the fact that he loves Georgiana and feels confident that his attempt to remove the birthmark will succeed. Thus at the same time that we recoil we can identify with Aylmer and through him act out some of our secret desires. . . . The story not only gives expression to impulses which are ordinarily repressed; it gives them a sympathetic hearing—an opportunity to show whether they can be gratified without causing trouble or pain. There are obvious gains in being able to conduct tests of this kind with no more danger and no greater expenditure of effort than is involved in reading a story." The one significant dissenting view is offered by Frederick Crews, *The Sins of the Fathers* (New York: Oxford University Press, 1966), whose scattered comments on the story focus on the specific form of Aylmer's idealism and its implications for his secret motives.

7. In the conventional reading of the story Georgiana's birthmark is seen as the symbol of original sin—see, for example, Heilman, p. 579; Bell, p. 185. But what this reading ignores are, of course, the implications of the fact that the symbol of original sin is female and that the story only "works" because men have the power to project that definition onto women.

8. Gornick and Moran, *Woman in Sexist Society*, p. 192.

9. Mary Daly, *Beyond God the Father*, p. 195. It is useful to compare Daly's analysis of "Male Mothers" with Ellmann's discussion of the "imagined motherhood of the male" in *Thinking About Women*, pp. 15ff. It is obvious that this myth is prevalent in patriarchal culture, and it would seem reasonable to suggest that the patterns of co-optation noticed in "Rip Van Winkle" and "I Want to Know Why" are minor manifestations of it. *An American Dream* provides a major manifestation, in fact a tour de force, of the myth of male motherhood.

10. See *Faulkner in the University: Class Conferences at the University of Virginia 1957-1958*, eds. Frederick L. Gwynn and Joseph L. Blotner (Charlottesville: University of Virginia Press, 1959), pp. 87-88; *Faulkner at Nagano*, ed. Robert A. Jeliffe (Tokyo: Kenkyusha Ltd., 1956), p. 71.

11. For a sense of some of the difficulties involved in reading the story in these terms, I refer the reader to the collection of criticism edited by M. Thomas Inge, *A Rose for Emily* (Columbus: Merrill, 1970).

CHAPTER 2

1. *Ernest Hemingway: An Introduction and Interpretation* (New York: Holt, Rinehart and Winston, 1967), p. 73.

2. Robert W. Lewis, Jr., "The Tough Romance" in *Twentieth Century Interpretations of "A Farewell to Arms,"* ed. Jay Gellens (Englewood Cliffs: Prentice-Hall, 1970), p. 45.

3. Philip Young, *Ernest Hemingway: A Reconsideration*, rev. ed. (New York: Harcourt, 1966), p. 93.

4. Susan Brownmiller's extended analysis of the role of war in encouraging and legitimizing rape is relevant here. See Chapter III of *Against Our Will: Men, Women and Rape* (New York: Simon and Schuster, 1975).

5. The suggestion that the Abruzzi is an ideal world because in it female sexuality is carefully controlled may be reinforced if we consider a possible context for the ban against flute playing. According to Joanne Edgar in "'Wonder Woman' Revisited," *Ms.* 1 (July, 1972), 52-56, one of the major elements in the mythology surrounding the legendary Amazon society of South America is the belief that "these fierce female warriors and powerful victors kidnapped males from neighboring tribes, and brought them to a copulatorium for a mating ritual complete with dancing and flute music." In the Abruzzi, "it was forbidden to play the flute at night. . . . Because it was bad for the girls to hear the flute at night" (p. 73). If this prohibition stems from the same association of female sexuality with flute music and the same vision of the danger to men of that sexuality as the myths about the Amazons, then the Abruzzi is indeed a version of that ideal American territory whose achievement is the implicit goal in *A Farewell to Arms*.

6. In this connection see Wyndham Lewis's essay on *A Farewell to Arms*, reprinted in *Twentieth Century Interpretations* (pp. 72-90) as "The 'Dumb Ox' in Love and War." In describing and ultimately decrying the paralysis of the will that characterizes the Hemingway protagonist, Lewis picks as his point of comparison and his representative of "passionate personal energy" Prosper Merimee's Don José, who dealt in a truly Othello-like way with his particular Desdemona, Carmen. In part, then, what Lewis's essay seems to be is a lament for the good old days when men's hostility toward women could be openly expressed and socially justified. Indeed, the politics of this change are, as Lewis implies, immense. See also the section on Hemingway in Gershon Legman's *Love and Death* (New York: Hacker Art Books, 1949), pp. 86-90, which begins, "No modern writer has taken the hatred of women farther than has Ernest Hemingway."

7. *Hemingway: The Writer's Art of Self-Defense* (Minneapolis: University of Minnesota Press, 1969), pp. 82-83.

8. Wyndham Lewis, pp. 73, 90.

9. *Hemingway and the Dead Gods* (Lexington: University of Kentucky Press, 1960), p. 47.

10. Lewis, pp. 52 and 53.

11. Gellens, p. 13.

12. *Hemingway: The Writer as Artist,* 3rd. ed. (Princeton: Princeton University Press, 1963), p. 113.

CHAPTER 3

1. For an extended analysis of this point, see Joanna Russ, "What Can a Heroine Do? or Why Women Can't Write," in *Images of Women in Fiction,* ed. Susan Koppelman Cornillon (Bowling Green: Bowling Green University Popular Press, 1972), pp. 3-20.

2. *The Letters of F. Scott Fitzgerald,* ed. Andrew Turnbull (1963; rpt. New York: Dell, 1966), pp. 366-67.

3. The plays on Daisy's name may also include the idea that she combines both the turning world and a safe center from which to observe it—the day's eye. And, in this connection, Leslie Fiedler's comments on the origins and meaning of Fitzgerald's romanticization of the rich are worth noting. According to Fiedler, Fitzgerald saw in the rich the possibility of "a perpetual area of freedom, like that in which the artist momentarily feels himself in the instant of creative outpouring." See "Some Notes on F. Scott Fitzgerald," in *An End to Innocence* (Boston: Beacon, 1955), p. 182.

4. One might wish to consider, in connection with this point, the implications of David Minter's comment that "behind Gatsby there is a history of dislocation and alienation, the attendants, as it were, of the experience of immigration." See "Dream, Design, and Interpretation in *The Great Gatsby,*" in *Twentieth Century Interpretations of "The Great Gatsby,"* ed. Ernest Lockridge (Englewood Cliffs: Prentice-Hall, 1968), p. 83.

5. "Handle With Care," in *The Crack-Up,* ed. Edmund Wilson (1945; rpt. New York: New Directions, 1956), p. 77. One might note that Fitzgerald's anger at Zelda for his being put in this position was compounded during the writing of *The Great Gatsby.* This was the period of Zelda's "affair" with the French flyer, which Fitzgerald interpreted as a betrayal of him and in large part an attempt to destroy his ability to work.

6. Reprinted in *Twentieth Century Interpretations,* p. 109.

7. See, for example, Arthur Mizener, *The Far Side of Paradise*, rev. ed. (Boston: Houghton Mifflin, 1965), pp. 185ff.; Thomas A. Hanzo, "The Theme and the Narrator of *The Great Gatsby*," *Modern Fiction Studies* 2 (1956-57), 183-90; Gary Scrimgeour, "Against *The Great Gatsby*," *Criticism* 8 (1966), 75-86; R. W. Stallman, "Gatsby and The Hole in Time," *Modern Fiction Studies* 1 (1955), 2-16.

8. Scrimgeour, p. 85.

9. Ibid., p. 81.

10. It is worth noting here, in partial support of the accuracy of this description of the psychological action of *The Great Gatsby*, that in the first conception of the novel Fitzgerald intended Nick to be in love with Daisy too. In subsequent revisions "Gatsby gradually emerged as a more innocent and sympathetic character than Fitzgerald had first conceived," and Nick has shifted his romantic interest from Daisy to Gatsby. See Henry Dan Piper, *F. Scott Fitzgerald: A Critical Portrait* (London: The Bodley Head, 1965), pp. 107ff.; p. 143.

11. *The Letters of F. Scott Fitzgerald*, p. 383.

12. Bewley, *The Eccentric Design* (New York: Columbia University Press, 1963), p. 276; Trilling, *The Liberal Imagination* (1950; rpt. Garden City: Anchor-Doubleday, 1953), p. 244; Troy, "Scott Fitzgerald—The Authority of Failure," *Accent* 6 (1945), reprinted in *F. Scott Fitzgerald: A Collection of Critical Essays*, p. 21; Dyson, "*The Great Gatsby:* Thirty-Six Years After," *Modern Fiction Studies* 7 (1961), 38.

13. Bewley, p. 278.

CHAPTER 4

1. We owe the identification of this creature, of course, to Mary Ellmann. See Chapter II of *Thinking About Women*.

2. Incidentally, Trilling gives a pretty clear idea of what he means by manhood, and what he fears the loss of, in commenting on the possible uses one could make of a hero from the West, James's original intention being to make Ransom a Westerner: "Such a hero might indeed be used to make a cultural-sexual point—in 1906 the Western hero of William Vaughn Moody's

The Great Divide was to rape the New England heroine for her own good; the audiences of Broadway were delighted with this show of benevolent violence. . . ."

3. This view of the novel is exemplified in Peter Buitenhuis's treatment of *The Bostonians* in *The Grasping Imagination* (Toronto: University of Toronto Press, 1970): "Ransom, of course, has survived the War, but he has seen many of his friends die and is himself a symbolic representative of defeat. He bears on his shoulders the whole burden of re-establishing (or ransoming) the male element in the life he sees around him. As such he fights against overwhelming odds" (p. 112).

4. Anderson, p. 321.

5. Quoted in "Portrait of Alice James," in *The Diary of Alice James*, ed. Leon Edel (New York: Dodd, Mead, 1934), p. 9.

6. Ibid.

7. Ibid., p. 10.

8. Quoted in "Portrait," p. 13.

9. Howe, Introduction, p. x.

10. *The American Stories and Novels of Henry James*, ed. F. O. Matthiessen (1947; rpt. New York: Knopf, 1964), xix-xx.

11. Trilling, p. 116.

CHAPTER 5

1. Frederic Jameson, "The Great American Hunter, or Ideological Content in the Novel," *College English* 34 (1972), 190.

2. Ibid., p. 186.

3. Mary Ellmann, *Thinking About Women* (New York: Harcourt Brace Jovanovich, 1968), p. 73.

4. Jameson, p. 193.

5. Kate Millett, *Sexual Politics* (Garden City: Doubleday, 1970), p. 314.

6. *Time*, 5 December 1960, p. 17.

7. George Alfred Schrader, "Norman Mailer and the Despair of Defiance," *Yale Review* 51 (1961); reprinted in *Norman Mailer: A Collection of Critical Essays*, ed. Leo Braudy (Englewood Cliffs: Prentice-Hall, 1972), p. 83.

8. Quoted in Schrader, pp. 82-83.

9. Quoted in Brock Brower, "Always the Challenger," *Life*, 24 September 1965, p. 102.

10. *Advertisements for Myself* (1959; rpt. New York: Berkley-Putnam, 1966), p. 312.

11. *New York Times*, 5 June 1968, p. 50.

12. Ibid.

13. Norman Mailer, *The Prisoner of Sex* (New York: Signet–New American Library, 1971), p. 47.

14. Ibid., pp. 35-36.

15. Ibid., pp. 111-12.

16. Millett, p. 327.

17. For the fullest account of this drama, see Daly, *Beyond God the Father*.

18. *Prisoner*, pp. 112, 86.